I0132709

The World According To AI

(It's Not What You Think)

Arno Ilic

Copyright 2023 by Arno Ilic

Prepared For Publication by Native Book Publishing

Table of Contents

11 Who Are We?

12 About Truth

13 Relationships

14 Life

INTRODUCTION

The world we inhabit today is filled with computers and other forms of electronic technology. In today's time, possibly more so than at any point in humanity's history, we have unfortunately lost our ability to accept things as they are. If they are in our power to fix them, we should. If we cannot rectify those things, we should find someone who can.

As a result, we have become a nation of whiners, complainers, and addictive consumers.

Change is brought into society through each individual's input and participation in their actions, whether revolutionary or visionary. However, we are still stuck in a saviour complex; we expect a hero to spring up and save us from our predicament. We vote for governments who will provide us with the benefits we think we need- we put ourselves first instead of the nation as a whole. We have forgotten how to be human. Some politicians want to be elected to fulfill their or their 'party's agenda to demonstrate a performative manner of care to placate and appease their constituents. Some politicians work for votes, not necessarily what is best for the country. Many participate in backdoor dealings that are not necessarily fulfilling the interests of the nation, but rather the latter's interests. In the end, neither side is happy,and the nation continues to suffer behind the desires of each opposing view. In a way, 'it's just a display of a power struggle.

The technological side has advanced exponenttially, but not the human species itself. In fact, much has remained the same since the times of Socrates. Many wise men and religious leaders have pointed the way, yet we continue disregarding the signposts. So, I don't believe our species has evolved at all.

I believe that we were raised that way: we were taught to surrender to our nefarious interests and needs over other people. We learn early on what buttons to push with parents. Most new parents get exacerbated when children whine and cry. All they want to do is stop them from crying or whining. At an early age, they recognize that the way to get things is to be annoying or intimidating. This goes into their memory bank.

It is the first step in programming. This software becomes refined (using our artificial intelligence) along the way because "stamping our feet and crying is not socially acceptable and is "childish." So, to adhere to the conforming environment, we updated our software. Instead of showing our frustration overtly, we resort to updating our methods by bullying, manipulating, yelling, or threatening others.

Many times, these behaviours seem to work, and people get a free pass due to their age, gender, or social position in society. However, it is mostly regarded as a negative association with our personalities. Even so, most humans have now reprogrammed this response to our "What Works" bucket of the brain. Conversely, if a parent disciplines or punishes a child that "misbehaves" (behaves as an average child would), the child may become introverted and learn that it is better to keep quiet. Some may allow themselves to be bullied, while others may become passive-aggressive.

Without notice, we are trying to create a machine like us – also a machine. We are becoming the ultimate artificial intelligence machine built on instructions and a predictive reactionary function. Ironically, the same humans do not think of themselves as machines. If you question them concerning this, they will act defensively and suggest that 'it's a lie, citing examples of how they are free thinkers. After all, we reason that humans have the ability to think. Thus, through emotions, we can discern between good and evil. A computer can't do the same, but is that really the truth? Machines are already programmed to accept logic, and intelligent computers can think and reason. So, what is the missing key that binds us to them? Emotions! You will be surprised to know that preprogrammed responses also drive emotions.

For instance, what may induce fear in one person may not produce the same reaction of fear in another person. Some people enjoy going through extreme adrenalin rushes while others do not. Someone can say "fuck you," and it immediately evokes a feeling of hostility, anger, and disrespect. They are just words we give meaning to and have no inherent importance or definition. In the same manner, we ascribe meanings to certain words of slang, and we could teach our computer to respond to those words too. For the moment, they are just words. But, with the addition of meaning, it can garner an emotive side to computers as well!

For example: Look at Valentine's Day. The colour we associate with it is red. That day is associated with red flowers, hearts, and decorations. February 14 is considered the day of love, and all celebrations, brand marketing, and displays are predominantly red. Yet, when viewed from a different perspective, red is also the colour of violence, anger, and even spirituality. Catholic priests wear red vestments during Pentecost Sundays and sometimes when they are ordained.

Furthermore, the Chinese believe that red connotes joy and luck. Conversely, the Spanish wear black for weddings, traditionally associated only with funerals in North America. Another blurred element is hidden between these examples, which is the variation of culture and its influence on our programming. Depending on where we're from, our culture programs us. We walk around thinking that we are correct and that the rest of the world is upside down.

When I came to this country as an immigrant, I was astonished and taken aback at the difference in culture. We had a particular way of doing things, which was quite different from our new homeland, and it created a strong question mark in my heart.

On top of this, we were poor; we bought all the things that butchers were discarding. In fact, a lot of things were given to us for free. We ate chicken livers, necks, hogs' feet and many other parts of an animal's anatomy that the North American culture was not used to.

The main reason was that our heritage belonged to Europe, and Europeans faced severe food scarcity after World War II. As a result, they learned to eat everything. Some of these things were turned into soups- pigs' feet into aspic. When people deal with a drastic change in habitat, lifestyle, or food, it is very tough to adapt to new surroundings. Not impossible, just challenging. Similarly, many North American foods didn't appeal to these war-ridden Europeans. However, as time passed, other cultures appeared from different continents and countries, and we adapted and began to like different foods. They also brought different religious beliefs with them. These things can separate us, and in many instances, they do. The varying differences also provide an opportunity to learn and look at religion from someone else's perspective.

Multitudes of people never leave their comfort zones; when someone comes out of their comfort zone, it's not something they are used to (colour, religion, culture, language etc.); they don't know how to cope, so they lash out on all these "foreigners."

Computers tend to work similarly. If, for instance, a computer is programmed with certain information, it will not recognize other information unless you tell it to. That means reprograming it.

The difference with Humans is that they tend to resist change. 'Change is an inherent system embedded in us by nature. The amygdala is a region of the brain that plays a key role in processing emotional information, including interpreting threats. Your physical self is actively defending you against transformation. This is why many individuals inside an organization may first push back against a novel effort or concept despite its obvious merits. They have emotional attachments to things, something that a computer does not (yet) have. We have not programmed it that way. Most of us can agree with the logic, although I am also questioning and pondering upon that. Emotions, on the other hand, as mentioned previously, are varied. There are no common feelings, so it becomes harder to program.

The purpose of saying all this is for the reader to recognize that they are stimulus-response machines because they are programmed to react to certain stimuli in specific ways.

For instance, if we wish to make more money, we tell our brains that we don't have sufficiency, so every action stems from that lack. Someone in a situation of poverty consciousness has that mindset, regardless of how rich or poor they are. Then someone tells them they should be positive, repeat affirmations that say I am rich and surround themselves with pictures of luxurious living. They do all these things, pay money for that "valuable" insight and wonder why they are no further ahead six months or a year later.

Saying affirmations do not work very well when the underlying thought is, "Really, I'm not rich" or, "yeah, but...." The power is in knowing; the Bible tells us (Mathew 21:22 King James Version) that it is in believing. While the Bible was written some time ago, there are iterations of translations. The actual wording should be "knowing." In other words, you can believe all you want that you are a millionaire; it 'doesn't mean you are. You know you are rich because you are. Priests say you must believe because they have no other explanation; they 'don't <u>know</u> either.

We must banish the doubt within us. Surprisingly, many people question if they are doing something right, whether it's practicing meditation, walking along a spiritual path, etc. This kind of thought process is what makes us similar to machines. We are looking for information outside ourselves that we have been taught from grade 1. For example, we read a book, and when asked what the book's premise is, the answer is either right or wrong. It has nothing to do with how we interpret or feel about the text individually. (Some good teachers will recognize individuality and thus allow for interpretation).

In addition to "Am I doing this right?" another similar question is "How?" This is a difficult question to answer. How do I breathe? Well, you can breathe either through your nose or mouth. Yes, but how do I do that? Just inhale. How do I do that? If you have never breathed, it would be difficult to fire up your brain signals to accommodate breathing. Because we not only learn to question but to receive answers, we fail to look within ourselves for answers.

Similarly, and perhaps a better example, is riding a bicycle. How do you do that? Sit on the seat and start pedalling. You might have to explain what pedals are, then talk about balance and how fast you need to pedal to maintain your balance. Then watch them fall.

These are little things we do not often think about. We rush through life without looking inward to understand life. We like others telling us what life is about. When I was younger, one of my daughters asked me for an answer to a mathematical word problem. I, in turn, asked her what the question was asking. Through a series of questions, I wanted her to discover the answer for herself. She became impatient and just "wanted the solution." That is the way kids are. (Note I did not say the younger generation. All generations have children. They act similarly.) If we do not teach them at a younger age, they will not want to figure out or develop the patience to answer themselves.

We might experience self-doubt from questioning anything about ourselves, including our beliefs, ideas, feelings, etc. The reactions of significant others to our decisions and blunders might often lead us to question our own abilities. Recognizing and accepting one's worth is one of the best ways to combat negative thoughts about one's abilities. It develops over time as you practise self-compassion and come to terms with your shortcomings while maintaining lofty goals.

When I was younger, I was taught about religious dogma and belief in the Bible. When I got older, I started to question several things. The response was that you just had to believe. Really? Just take your word for it. When something did not make sense, I started to look elsewhere for answers. Answers where someone didn't merely say, "Trust me." The knowing is in oneself, not in others. Russian Television had a saying, "Question more." That is good advice, but the questions should be intelligent.

This book can provide some insights into reprogramming your thoughts to increase your happiness and even tap into your inner peace of mind. Then again, it may not. You see, reading about something doesn't get you there. You must put in the work. Everyone, whether they admit it or not, is on the hunt for a sense of joy. It's a fundamental motivation for most human actions. Take a moment to consider your regular routine. Are there things you purposefully engage in that bring you down? Whenever you get up, do you ever think to yourself, "I can't wait to be unhappy today!" (Note that I am talking about "joy" and not happiness. Happiness tends to be driven by external stimuli, whereas joy comes from deep within.)The first step toward enlightened existence is realizing that being joyful is always the driving force. A few of the values that people strive to embody every day include honesty, integrity, love, and joy. However, values like health, wealth, celebrity, position, intellect, and so on are considered to be route values since they are important in achieving the perceived ultimate values.

Years ago, I took a course in TM (Transcendental Meditation). While practicing this for some years, I eventually found my way to a different meditation form. I studied various disciplines to conclude I am who I am. Over the years, I found out that there is no magic bullet. What can I do to get it right, or what is the fastest way to get results? It is akin to a vegetable plant asking when I will produce vegetables or the child in the back seat asking, "Are we there yet?" The answer, of course, is that the plant will have vegetables when it does, and not before. The child will arrive when it does, and not any earlier.

We fail to understand that we grow as humans, whether emotionally or spiritually. We don't get there any faster because our mind tells us to. We do not contemplate the other consideration that we all grow at different rates. Just as some plants take longer to bloom, so do humans. Some never produce flowers, and they were never meant to. They serve different purposes. Humans should find their own way and see what they can contribute to the planet. No matter the circumstances of their genesis, living things, most of them, if not all, are special in their own unique manner.

One thing we fail to recognize is that this is one planet. If we cannot get along, we will never do so. I am always saddened by how we think of ourselves first. For instance, there is the COVID-19 vaccine. Many are scrambling to be the first in line. God forbid that a politician would have the audacity to share the vaccine with other nations because of their misfortune. Those politicians would most likely not get re-elected. What makes us more special than other human beings? I have been to places in India where people are far less fortunate than homeless people in North America. We do not look after the poor in our developing countries. Nor do we prioritize our indigenous people (that we displaced) who lack proper mental and physical healthcare, education, or water. Until and unless we start focusing on the neediest, we simply cannot progress as a society. We fail to evolve because of our programming. If we perceive ourselves as lacking in our lives, we will never focus on 'others.' We need to shift our perspective from me to include the neighbourhood, the county, province or state, country, continent and finally, the planet. After all, we are all in this together. Perhaps if we looked at "me" and "I" as plural instead of singular, we might see "us" as needing the basics first.

Selfishness, however, is not something that has to be quantified. The truth is that you, I, and everyone else on this planet all think about ourselves first. 'It's an instinct. It might be hard for some individuals to accept that they are just as self-centred as everyone else on Earth. Individuals prefer to believe that they are really selfless and that everyone else is selfish. Do we not, in the end, simply care about ourselves? According to psychology studies, the reverse is true; people's self-interest is not their fundamental motivator. Numerous studies have shown that people often prioritize the group's interests above their own. Still, the majority does end up being self-centred in the modern era.

When we point at others to say they are different or they don't belong, we are really shifting the focus from us so that others look elsewhere. If they look at us, they may see our faults; it is best to point at other people's failings. And, who better to redirect to than someone visibly different from us?

I have compiled some topics in this book, answering questions others might be interested in. I thought they might be helpful, as many questions have a similar theme.

1

AWARENESS

The key to growth is the introduction of higher dimensions of consciousness into our awareness.

Lao Tzu

I

THE MIND

Now, the journey towards greater awareness and self-discovery is an experience we have alone, and it cannot be shared or studied out of a book. Instead, it comes from interacting with people while observing our reactions to various events, circumstances, actions, or other's points of view. Reflection and introspection allow one to develop a level of self-awareness characterized by clarity and objectivity.

Silence comes from within. I have found that being centred will assist with silence. However, we have no control over our thoughts. We have many ruminations, those we pay attention to and those almost unaware. Learning to let go of our constant thoughts will quieten the mind. Years ago, I would fast for a week without anything except organic juices and water. I noticed that for the first couple of days, my mind was going non-stop about how hungry I was and, "can't I just have something - what is the harm?" "You are doing damage to your system." After about the third day, my mind started to get extremely quiet. The brain was worried that I might die or never get fed again. In fact, I found that my energy level increased, and I had clarity of mind because there was little to no chatter.

Now, you do not have to go to those extremes. Do not give energy to your thoughts by trying to resist them. I can sit in meditation, and in the past, I have noticed that although my thoughts were gone, I observed a ringing sensation coming through my ears. Eventually, that, too, went away. In a long-winded way, I am saying, leave your thoughts be. They will come and go. You will find stillness when you look into your heart (mine emanates from my solar plexus). You will discover much silence if you continually go back to that area.

We are no longer uninformed if we access our "unconscious" mind. This becomes mingled with your conscious mind, which interprets what you already know; thus, you may experience confusion with your conscious mind. There is more clarity to our knowledge when we get beyond our conscious minds. We cannot accelerate our learning faster than our experiences. In other words, we may learn many things, but we will only know them conceptually (isn't that what philosophy is about? Ruminating things through the mind and stating them as meaningful ideas without ever having experienced those things,) instead of experientially. We understand how to ride a bicycle but will not experience it until we ride it. We will not understand what our unique experience in the riding may produce. It could be one of unbridled exhilaration or pure panic. It can be the joy of seeing the countryside on a beautiful day or the agony of trying to get home in a downpour while our legs are yelling for us to stop pedalling.

Meditation is a powerful tool and has been used throughout the ages. Calm, tranquilly, and equilibrium are all things that may be gained through meditation, and all of these things have positive effects on your mental and physical health. As an added bonus, you may utilize it to help you unwind and deal with stress by shifting your focus to something soothing. The practice of meditation may teach you how to calm your mind and find equilibrium.

Being mindful is one of the most straightforward and challenging things to do. Our mind wants us to focus on everything but the here and now. Being mindful is all about the here and now. When we are aware, we are totally absorbed in what we are doing. Simply said, mindfulness is the state of mind in which a person is not unduly reactive to or overwhelmed by the events and stimuli in their immediate environment.

Although the capacity for mindfulness is inherent in every human being, it may be developed further by regular practice.

Mindfulness is the act of intentionally paying attention, either to external stimuli via the senses or internal ones through the mind and emotions. More and more studies are revealing that the physical structure of the brain may be changed via the practice of mindfulness.

Years ago (before everything was online), I used to prepare for arbitration cases. I would leave the house at 9:00 am on a Sunday, telling my wife I would be back in three to four hours. Ten hours later, my wife would call and ask if I was coming home for supper. I had no idea that so much time had passed. I was totally immersed in research with nothing else on my mind.

If someone wants to be "more mindful," are they not already aware? Otherwise, how would they know they want to be "more" mindful?

It will become much more evident by staying in the moments of thinking and doing. Everything happens with continued practice. Put away your app. You don't need it. It is just something to spend money on. Here's the thing; you are already mindful of what you need to do. For instance, when you first moved into new living quarters, you had to know your floor and apartment number. If you have a house, you must become aware of where the kitchen, the family room, etc. exists. You must be mindful of how you get from home to work and vice versa. Once you know all of this, it becomes automatic, and you no longer think about it (that is, you become mindless).

If you look at things for the first time constantly, you become much more adept at mindfulness. I used to tell my staff that they needed to look at things as though they were doing it for the first time. It forces them to become more mindful of what they do. It causes you to ask more and better questions. What is the purpose of doing this? Is it necessary? Can we do this better?

Become mindful of the food you eat. Bite into a tomato, and before you do, note its colour and the skin's smoothness. What does it taste like? What was the initial reaction to your teeth? Look at the seeds. How are they placed within the tomato? Take a seed and taste it. How was it—think of the texture. What colour was it? Did it taste bitter?

By doing this, you become more mindful. Pretty soon (months or years), you will notice that you are forming a mindfulness habit. Sometimes, we forget and go back into our pattern of mindlessness, but we are moving forward. A single step on a 10 km walk doesn't seem like you are going anywhere. After several thousand footprints, you turn around and notice that you are far from where you started. Change is subtle.

II
LAYERS

We have grown as onions, adding layers at every turn. We start by becoming insecure at a relatively early age. I watched our children and grandchildren develop. They start learning about what is and isn't acceptable to do. They know this mainly through their parents but also their peers. Religion is taught (more or less dictated), so we tend to adjust ourselves to fit into that society. If we cannot explain something, then it just requires "faith." Schools teach us rudimentary forms of what the world demands of us to become "valuable" citizens. (I remember a science teacher who couldn't explain a formula he had on the board. His answer was "you don't question what 4X3 is; you just accept that it is 12. Same with this formula, you just have to accept it." Wouldn't it be better to say, "I don't know, and I'll get you the answer tomorrow"). Here is a person who should be teaching us how to create formulas, yet he teaches you to accept things without logic.

We learn to take advantage of one another, make money, and look with envy upon "successful" people. It's a false dilemma created by the society we live within that bounds people to appreciate and indulge in a cat-and-mouse chase to wealth and the prosperity associated to it. In the end, who are we if not clad in branded clothes and shoes, buying into more materialism to fill in the empty spaces of our hearts? We cultivate an image and lie to maintain it: we continue the tradition throughout our lives. It never ends, does it? Each iteration adds another layer to the onion. We are soon removed so far from our core that we no longer know who we are. If computers are improperly programmed, they may be in a continual loop or not function as required. It happens to humans as well.

I sometimes chuckle when I hear people talk about enlightenment. I refrain from mentioning how dumb their questions seem, as I was on that path. When we remove the onion's first layer, we seek approval that we are doing things the "right way." It gets more teary-eyed (painful) as we clear away more layers. Those beliefs that we have harboured are far below the surface and ingrained. We have also learned to bury experiences we are not comfortable with. After all, our lives are working. We're okay. It is the rest of society that is screwed up. I study what people say. It leads me to what they are lacking. "I need more money," tells me they have a lack in their lives. "That person disrespected me" indicates that they lack self-respect, and so on.

There are so many layers of being human. There is no end to peeling all the layers until we reach nothing. It is only at that point that we realize everything. If we are lucky enough to be still living, we forget it all and continue with the memory of knowing everything and nothing simultaneously. Peeling our layers away also reflects the peeling of an onion. The first outer layers are the easiest to remove. The more you peel away, the harder it gets. It's the same with life. We tend to delude ourselves into thinking we are "enlightened" or ahead of others, making us much wiser. As we continue peeling, we realize we are only touching the surface. If we think we are better than, or more enlightened, or above the fray, we still have many layers to shed.

Our thoughts are so preoccupied with the past and the future that we hardly ever pay attention to the here and now. We fail to appreciate our own being here on this amazing Earth, and we seldom pause for introspection. Because of this, the days begin to blend together. Daily, we encounter a barrage of stimuli from which we can hardly make sense. So, while we struggle to make sense of the universe, we fail to see that life contains more than we had ever dreamed.

We're all here on Earth for our own personal reasons and to have our own individual adventures. Our aspirations may be different, but our similarities are equally important. Human needs, including the want for a rich experience in life.

Layer one allows us to experience the inestimable value of human life. In that split second, we demonstrate our individuality by providing the world with our own distinct perspective and context.

The next layer, however, is where we find purpose in life and, if in the first we took use of the gift of being alive, in the second layer we took advantage of the good fortune of being human and evoked our desires and out our dreams to rest, by completing them of course.

Sometimes, we allow our circumstances to dictate what we do, how we react, and how we enable interference to sidetrack our spiritual development.

Depending on our "programming," sometimes we fail to evaluate our response before diving into a solution. Within that moment, we forget who we are and instinctively react to how we have been programmed. Depending on how our "software" has been compiled, we may never get beyond being a stimulus/response machine.

There is a fine line between allowing them to express themselves and balancing that with social acceptability when raising children. We had four children, and each was brought up slightly differently. The first child had it the hardest because we wanted to prove to our parents that we could also be good parents. (We tend to need approval when doing something new). The last one got our wisdom through the experiments from those that preceded her. What is most important for the child is what really matters, not what we want from them. When I watch my kids raise theirs, I sometimes bite my tongue.

III
Awakening

We think an awakened person no longer has to cook, do laundry, or work. Those who think like that may also believe that the rest of humanity is beneath them. In fact, being awakened helps us understand that everything is transitory. People still die and suffer, and life's circumstances will not change. What great leaders teach; is to reduce stress by acceptance. What causes us tension is wanting what we don't have and not being satisfied with what we have. Living outside the present moment is another stressor. One becomes "awake" when they stop seeing the world through the lens of their ego and stop dwelling on the past and the future. As an alternative, you have a near-simultaneous sense of both your unique identity and your place in the greater scheme of things.

Anything can be done mindfully; you just have to decide to be that way. We do things in a state of awareness when we do something for the first time. After the tenth time, we no longer think about it and become "mindless."

When you walk, do you notice how you put one foot in front of the other? What does it feel like when the front of your foot lands on the sidewalk or floor? Do you put your heel down first? Does your foot roll in or out when placed on the ground?

When you listen to someone talking, are you really listening, or are you just waiting for the person to finish, so you can say the next thing that pops into your head?

What kinds of thoughts are you having right now? Are they an expression of your highest self? If not, what kinds of judgements have you made about your deliberations?

You see, there are many ways to be mindful.

It takes a long time to achieve what one seeks fully. I suggest meditation if you are not already doing that. Reading books on Zen is another way to advance. However, you only get the "intellectual" version when you read from a book. Experience comes through doing and practice. Understanding how to be calm and Zen-like is not the same as being that. To remain calm all the time takes a great degree of discipline and practice. Some things still annoy me. The difference is that I can let go of those annoyances a lot quicker than years ago. Continue to live in each moment and be mindful of all you do. It is not possible to be that way 100% of the time, nor even 50% at times. When you see yourself thinking about the past or the future, gently go back to the present. There is no need to beat yourself up if you don't.

As I was starting to "wake up," I became insufferable. I thought I knew everything and tried to convince everyone of my point of view. Today, I allow people to be who they are and understand that they are on a journey and moving at their own pace. I still work. I encounter many different people from different walks of life and beliefs. I do the tasks related to what I do with joy and enthusiasm. It was not always like that. I would worry about what others thought of me. When is my next promotion, and so on? I realized that none of this mattered. When I bring joy and happiness to what I do, I am already where I want to be. When you stop thinking about your past and future, you stop seeing the world through the filter of your ego, and you become awake. You, on the other hand, feel like you have a firm grasp on both your individuality and your role in the grand scheme of things at almost the same time.

IV

JUDGEMENT

So long as you are in the judgement of people, you cannot claim to be spiritually awakened. Sometimes old books can be helpful, but be cautious, as they can only point in a direction. Even the bible points to not judging unless you are prepared to pronounce a sentence on yourself. First of all, there is no such thing as a devil. The devil that resides in each of us is our thoughts. Spiritual leaders who talk about evil people are the worst. They judge all the time. How can they be teachers if they have not reached that level of spiritual awareness? Besides, being aware is one thing; practicing is entirely different.

If you consider yourself spiritually awakened, you still have a long way to traverse. Many years ago, I suffered (actually, the people I was trying to explain my awakening to that really suffered) through what some of you may be going through or are the recipient of today. We start to awaken and don't understand why other people don't get it or aren't in the same place. We tend to judge people in that manner. Why can't they just behave? Why must they always argue? Some people are simply dumb. When I read *Neale Walsh's* book Conversations With God, it described how people are in various evolving stages. It would be akin to teaching a grade two student algebra. Just because you know and understand algebra doesn't make the grade 2 student evil or stupid. They simply lack your learning and experience.

Similarly, large swaths of the population see things without context; they make assumptions based on their programming and memory storage. I believe it was Deepak Chopra who said that if you go into a train station or an airport, it looks like utter chaos. Yet, people know precisely where they want to go.

Prejudice is about pre-judging. We make assumptions about people without really knowing them. We see nightly news of people of colour being arrested and immediately mistrusting all. Even if we see lawyers, doctors or other highly successful people, we put them into the bucket of "those are the minority." Then we can continue our line of pre-judging.
A person may, for instance, have many negative stereotypes about Christians, Muslims, and Jews, and these beliefs may colour how they interact with others of these faiths. Likewise, it's possible for individuals of different races to have the same experiences. Similarly, we see police officers abusing or killing people simply because of the colour of their skin. We instantly paint all police with the same brush and mistrust them all; this does not negate the fact that institutions are systemically biased. Again, we cannot paint all institutions with the same brush. But all should review their policies and procedures to ensure they are accommodating.

Let's try to understand the person talking; we may get a glimpse of another perspective. Think of seeing a three-dimensional object. Mostly what we see is a two-dimensional view of the subject. Each time someone adds information, we broaden our perspective; we get closer to seeing the authentic picture, the third dimension, if you will.

The most challenging thing about seeing another point of view is to allow ourselves to be open to seeing it without judgment. Even if the person you are talking to spews nonsense, take the time to listen. What was the source of his information? How did he come to their conclusions? Are they accurate or partially so on the balance of probability? If they have it half right or just twenty-five percent, which portion will you keep? Even if they are only two percent accurate, you are now two percent ahead of where you were.

Someone asked me whether I favoured relaxing over overworking. I responded by saying, I bring joy to everything I do. Work and Relaxing are opposite sides of the same coin. When preferring one over the other, we judge one over the other.

For instance, when working, the entire focus should be on work. When focused, there are few distractions. It's called "being in the zone." When relaxed and reading, I am totally immersed in the book.

We need to work to keep our bodies and brains functioning. We need to relax so that our bodies and brains can recharge themselves. They are dependent on each other to function correctly. Having a favourite becomes a bit silly when thinking about it. Getting the most out of work becomes difficult when done begrudgingly. Do it with enthusiasm and joy. Decide that before starting the task; even if you don't know where to start, just start; the rest comes naturally.

To stay in decent shape, office workers need to find time for exercise. Go to the gym. Just get the body moving to keep both body and mind sharp.

If all we do is work from early in the morning until late at night, our bodies may wear out. On the other hand, if we do nothing but relax, our bodies will atrophy. We really need a balance of both. Why not choose to enjoy what you are doing instead of doing it with drudgery?

V
THE SOUL

You may think of your soul as the part of you that contains your mind, personality, ideas, and emotions. There is a widespread belief that the soul survives physical death. It's the intangible part of a person that gives them their unique identity and humanity, sometimes used interchangeably with "mind" or "self" in religious and philosophical contexts.

The soul does not have bad qualities; the soul is the purest form of being. It does not judge. When you are in touch with that, you will notice only an observance and no judgment. It is the mind that does all that. The mind thinks there is such a thing as an evil soul. No, the brain determines if we are talking about good or evil. Not the soul. To put a finer point on that, your mind is like a computer, garbage in, garbage out. Thus, you become the machine driven by the brain, the software. Then you will notice how you defend yourself and say, no, I am not a machine. I have free will, which a material device doesn't; your mind has totally been deceived. The ego is now defending itself. It is unknown within you unless you continually explore the mind and how it reacts to situations. Ask why you are fearful in non-threatening settings. Is that the mind or the soul? The soul is universal. As a result, if it is afraid, then the entire universe would be fearful. It is not the soul. It is your programming that invites anxiety, your computer.

VI
PAST LIVES

Someone asked me about past lives some time ago. I am not the person to ask, as I do not believe in them. For me, there are no past or future lives. They are an illusion of the mind. Your history, and for that matter, all history, exists in minds and books. It is the same place the future lies. I admit this is a complex concept to accept. After all, you interacted with parents and friends who may have passed. Many people talk about past lives, including Eastern philosophy. If you close your eyes and think of a past life, your mind will develop an image. Is it a past life or a vision based on historical information in your memory bank? Looking to the past or future for answers causes us the most anxiety. That is because we are not aligned with the present. For argument's sake, let us assume you had a past life. Now what? Better still, so what! You talk about Karma, which is why you turned out the way you did. Well, which is it? Do you have free will, or are you a machine influenced by past lives, i.e., programming? It is a great way to abdicate responsibility for your behaviour, isn't it?

I remember reading about out-of-body experiences many years ago, and I thought practicing it would be cool. I even took a weekend class on how to do it. While working on it, I thought, "so what?" How will my ability to travel outside my body enhance my fellow human, or me, for that matter? Whenever you do something, ask yourself what the end game is. If it is just inquisitiveness and curiosity for the sake of an enquiring mind, then perhaps you should start to delve into your need to know. What made matters worse is that the person giving the lecture talked about how he would go out of the body and then have cyber-sex with women who were also having out-of-body experiences. Not only did

I think it was immoral (he was married), but if that was all to be done, then no thanks. The juveniles in the room were fascinated by the idea.

VII
FINDING ONESELF

There really is only one of you. You may be under a mistaken belief that there is more than one being. This is a misconception. We look to find our "true self" for some reason. If I took an apple tree from seed to fruition, do we ask which stage of the tree's development is its true self? Surely not! A tree, or for that matter, any living thing, is its whole being. Do we change over the years, of course? It doesn't mean that one aspect of our life is more authentic than another. The apple tree is an apple tree from seedling to maturity. The fact that it grows apples instead of oranges is known at birth. Your essence is also known at birth. This delusion of ourselves prevents us from seeing ourselves or others as holistic. We have programmed our children from birth to look at the difference in our physicality. "You are special, different from those across the street, smarter, dumber, etc."

I had heard a lot about finding yourself. Many people have gone to faraway places to "find themselves," only to discover that their "self" is within. There is no "out there." So, it was mostly my inner being that drove me to where I could go to connect to myself. So, that was to attend a meditation class. I read books on Buddhism. I read the Bible (twice), and those are the things that pointed me back to myself. Reading a book and attending seminars only pointed towards a direction.

I had to do the rest myself. It is the experiential component that brought me deeper within myself. Trekking through the Himalayas and Andes deepened that experience. However, by then, I had already realized that I did not need to "find myself." I was simply on a trek. It was an emotional experience, to be sure, but the rest of the group I was with did not "find themselves" either. Then again, none of us went there for anything other than an adventure. We crossed a mountain path where several wise spiritual teachers (gurus) were buried in one location. It was incredibly serene, and I felt quite emotional in that area. We had gone where tourists do not travel, so those parts of the mountains were quiet to start with.

So, is there a need to go anywhere to try and find yourself? No! You are already there. What you might wish to do instead is peel off the layers built up over the years. As we grow, we take in information from our parents, friends, peers, and teachers. We learn to protect ourselves from others by keeping our emotions within us. We show one side to work colleagues, another to friends, and yet another to parents and children.

Is it any wonder that we lose sight of who we are? That is why I mentioned that we have layers to peel off to get to who we are. In a way, there is no place to go but within. Think of a coin buried in the snow. The coinage is there, but you may not see it until you clear away the snow. If you set off to find the coin in the snow and return four months later when the snow has melted, you may think that you must go away for some time to see it. Yet, the coin has been there all this time.

VIII
QUESTIONING

When asked a "why" question, sometimes the answer came back as, "Because!" Does it really matter? Why does someone steal or kill? The "why" is not important, as knowing the reason itself may not prevent the act from happening. Our minds need to justify the actions we initiate. So, we make up stuff to satisfy the mind and our conscience. Most times, we are entirely unaware of why we do things. We do them impulsively. Then we have to make up a reason; that is where the "why" question comes into play. This consciousness manifests itself when we are cognisant of inquiries. We need to understand the relevance instead of simply responding to satisfy the questioner. When asking a "why" question, you are addressing the mind. When asking, "what" questions, you are addressing something deeper within.

Finding out the "why" of things gets you no closer to the truth. Why do people walk? It is not because of anything other than "because we walk." There is no "because we want to cross the street" or "visit family." Those are thoughts we use to justify walking. Besides, that is better answered by the "where" question.

As humans, we always need to explain our actions and behaviours. Imagine someone asking, "Why are you so aware?" You will feel compelled to provide a logical answer. If, for instance, you answer, "Because I am aware," that answer will not be good enough. We need reasons to satisfy our curiosity. Most "why" questions are not asked because we genuinely want to know; instead, they question our sanity. In other words, "Why are you always late?" has nothing to do with genuinely wanting to know. What you are really saying is, "be on time." Why not ask, "Is there something preventing you from being on time?" You really don't care why a person is late; you are more interested in ensuring they can be on time. You may be able to assist with that. Other questions can include: "Why is your fridge so full?" Depending on your motive for asking the question, there are more precise ways of asking. We could say, "I note your fridge is quite full; was there a sale," or "Are you having a party?" "Why do you walk," can be asked as: "do you walk for health reasons or because you cannot afford a ride? Or "where are you going?" These questions force the listener to answer more precisely and satisfy the questioner's curiosity.

Now, if you responded, "Because I investigated for years, read all the books on awareness and studied on a mountaintop with a guru," only then will you have satisfied the questioner. That doesn't mean that wisdom came from those places, but they did point to them.

IX
BEING MINDFUL

You may not be mindful of what you eat or how much you eat. When you realize you are not aware, you become conscious again. Eat slowly and pay attention when your body tells you that it has had enough. Being mindless causes us to put bad food into our bodies and overfill ourselves. Mindfulness applies to everything we do. Whenever you notice that you are not observant, return your attention to what you are doing.

To start, pick a fruit of some sort. When you're selecting an apple, note the colour of the skin. Are there multiple colours? Does one colour fade into the next? Are there red and yellow, and pink colours or different hues of green? Next, check out the texture of the skin. Is it smooth? Does it have bumps? When looking at them, notice if you judge any of their characteristics.

Look at the stem next; what colour is it? Is it hard? Does it have a knob on the top, or is it straight? If you decide to peel the apple, can you do so without breaking the peel? Did you start at the top or bottom? What caused you to start there? Take a look at the calyx,(the underside pedals of the apple, either green or turned brown), and what comes to mind? Cut the apple in half, lengthwise. Look at the inside. Note the mesocarp's different textures (the core's flesh). Then notice the endocarp (the hardened part around the seeds). Look at the seeds next. Check out the size and colour. When you bite into one, what is the taste sensation you get? (Note: eating too many seeds may cause nausea and vomiting. Beyond that, it may kill you). For this experiment, though, you should be fine. Was that bitter?

How about biting into the endocarp, the mesocarp? What sensations do you get?

After that, take a bite out of the flesh of the apple. Notice its texture when biting into it. How does it vary from the other parts of the apple?

When you have finished with this practice, you have been mindful. Everything you have felt and tasted with your senses is being conscious. Now, you can apply this experience to everything you do. You will then be in a constant state of awareness.

When that happens, your unconsciousness turns to consciousness. In other words, you become mindful of what is underneath the "aware" mind.

I have found at least two layers of an aware mind. First, there is the mind that talks to you all the time. It is like talking to yourself only without vocalizing it out loud. Then there is a quieter mind, which also has thoughts flowing, but you must be tuned to listening to it. It becomes clearer once your mind stops talking to you. These subtler thoughts may be interpreted as the source people think of as the "unconscious" mind. It can be said that those people are unaware of their quieter minds.

In that vein, we sometimes question ourselves about being perfect. Of course, perfection is simply the mind thinking we should be perfect in all we do and be Christ-like, Muhammad-like, Buddha-like, or any other religious leader-like. These people have evolved into the state they became. We have responsibilities to families, work, society and so on. That doesn't mean that we are "perfect" compared to others, but we are perfect within ourselves. Many thought Christ to be an agitator in the day. If He looked, He may have had inner doubts about things He could do differently. We simply don't know; we don't always convey our inner thoughts or misgivings.

People are already perfect. We jail them if they commit criminal acts for our protection. Don't condemn them, as it is not our place or right to do so. The law takes care of them, and we should be okay with that. Unfortunately, everyone who does something good or bad (to give these things a name), including us, does so, thinking they are entirely justified. We don't know what made them do something that we, as a society, disapprove of, but that doesn't mean that we cannot continue understanding them or even understanding that they are an expression of us.

X
STRESS

When we feel pressured or threatened, we respond with stress. The feeling of helplessness often arises when confronted with a circumstance we feel we cannot handle. Experiencing stress may happen on several different levels: the individual, such as when juggling a heavy workload, or the group, when dealing with a challenging situation.

I was given an assignment that had repercussions throughout the country, implementing a change management strategy; I was both anxious and stressed over the enormity of the task. However, once I started focusing on what was required right now and stayed in that mode through the entire project, the stress dissipated. That insight of "What needs to be done right now?" results from meditation. This mindfulness of only focusing on this moment made me realize I needed to focus on this moment.

We can minimize our stress by meditating, but for immediate relief, try focusing on whatever you are doing now. For instance, try not to think of anything else while reading this. Then, when done, think of the next task and go ahead and do that.

This also ties in with the book, "The Power of Now" by Eckhart Tolle. It is essentially about living in the present moment. When we do that, stress becomes a non-factor.

Too often, we become overwhelmed by the enormity of a situation. For instance, I don't look at what still needs to be cut when I cut the grass. Instead, I look to see what has already been cut. When working on a problem that may require weeks of work before it is completed, I look at what I can do right now. I plan for what needs to happen in the coming days and weeks, and then I forget about it and focus on this instant of time. Otherwise, we could get discouraged by the enormity of the tasks.

XI
THINKING

There is a school of thought that suggests thoughts are like radio waves. If you are in tune with them, you may confuse them with your own thinking. (See "Your Brain is a Radio," Radboud University Nijmegen, 2014) There is also other research. Check this one out in the New Science Newsletter of October 25, 1997, titled "Radio Head – The brain has its own FM receiver," by Alison Motluk.

Another level of thought comes from the same source as feelings emanate from. This thought is a different form of communication; it is more of a natural knowing and is always masked with what I will call your "brain thoughts." It is this more profound awareness that some will refer to as the spirit or pure consciousness. It is the source of knowledge that has no judgement attached to you or anyone or anything else.

Our thoughts are intrinsically pure. So, what is causing the impurities? Where do they come from? We can only answer this by studying our thoughts. Once we know what the "impurities" are, they still become essential in dealing with them. Shining a light into the darkness causes the darkness to vanish. The struggle will always be there if the light is in doubt. The night only comes when the sun visits the other side of the world. Your internal darkness, the impurities of the mind, happens when your awareness is not on the mind's thoughts but on some future event. The dark thoughts will recede and vanish when you shine a light onto your thoughts once more. The sun vanishes the darkness with its light; it does not judge the blackness as good or evil, nor does it order the tenebrosity to go away. It simply shines the light.

Darkness does the rest. So, too, it is with our thoughts. The awareness is the light. The attentiveness does not require anything else; it does not need to order your deductions to stop or judge your ruminations. It is only aware. That is, it shines the light. If you are walking along train tracks and become aware that a train is coming, you can take corrective action by getting off the train track. Similarly, when you are aware of your thinking, you can decide to alter how you wish to proceed. You can choose to "get off the tracks" or blame the train for being on it.

We wish our minds to be pure. In so doing, we evaluate that having a pure mind is good. Therefore, we become attached to the notion of needing a pure mind. This is another form of attachment and is not pure mind. It is a concept of a pure mind.

There are also questions on how to have an ideal mind. What may be perfect will be different for all of us. That's because we have different versions of what the model looks like. Since our mind deals with illusions, we know there is no ideal other than what we set. All we can do is our best with the information we have at the time. As someone once said, don't confuse the cereal box (picture of the ideal) with what is inside (the reality). Achieve your objectives, not what an ideal version of our dreams should be. Sometimes, we go through life thinking that we want to be happy, and that picture shows us with 2 children, perhaps a white picket fence and a shiny new car in the driveway. So, we think we have that yet to attain. But, when we look at ourselves, we realize we are already happy. Joy comes from within and has nothing to do with our image of what should be.

Christians are fond of saying, "What would Christ do?" and we should be more Christ-like. No. You are not Christ and cannot be Him, Moses, or anyone else. You are you; there is no one else like you. Be your best. It is all you can do. Small people judge. Don't be small, and don't allow small people to influence you.

Individual people are weak, but collectively, they are strong. Entire Eastern Europe's communist regime collapsed without bloodshed or meddling from other countries. It is time we stopped thinking about war and started looking at other means to resolve conflicts. This includes struggles within ourselves. It is time influential countries stop meddling in other counties' affairs, especially when they don't understand the culture. This includes intervening on a personal level. Perhaps we should be offering ways for the disenfranchised to become part of the mainstream. That would apply to countries and individuals. There may be a lot less animosity that eventually leads to war.

XII
LEARNING

Everything is hard when we have never done something before. It can be challenging to discipline ourselves, even for exceptionally talented people, because being proficient at something and having the discipline as well as the tenacity to learn about it are two very different things.

When you observe babies learning to crawl and subsequently walk, each action they take is challenging. They may take days or weeks to transition from laying to sitting to standing to walking. When they first learn to sit, they tend to topple over. When they take their first steps, they may fall into their parents' arms after taking a step or two. Then, they gradually learn to walk with practice until that act is no longer in their consciousness; it is simply instinct.

The difference between a child and an adult is that the adult has acclimated to instant gratification. A child doesn't wonder, "When will I ever learn this walking thing?" No, they persevere. We, as adults, should learn to do the same.

Fairy tales aside, we have human experiences. Those experiences may vary from person to person. But during our lifetime, as Werner Erhard said some time ago, "We do precisely what God wants us to do." I leave it up to the reader to determine who God is to them. When we die, some energy will dissipate back into the unknown. You notice I didn't say universe because that would imply another place. As we know, the universe holds the physical reality. A phrase that resonates with me is one that Deepak Chopra once used, calling it "The field of infinite possibilities." (If he didn't say it, then I'll take credit for it unless someone else said it before Deepak). Those are just the laws of physics. When we die, so does our universe, as we have perceived it.

All our experiences come together so that we are one. The mistake is thinking there is another physical place to go to or that "in my next life, I will be better." How is this exactly known? Things are passed on to us by spiritual leaders or parents. Still, realistically speaking, they don't know any more than you or I. Only reality cannot be fully explained. Even if we do come back, we come back in a different form with memories that may reside in quarks or other forms of energy. So, "how can we really know? If we factor in that time is an illusion, how do we know, or not know, that the person sitting across from us isn't really us, sitting in the same time and space, having a different experience.

I look at people in their forties and fifties with some skepticism when they promote certain lotions or potions that make them younger, or when they say that if you follow a particular practice, you can live longer. The ego's arrogance makes one think one can be immune to death. It is fear that drives us to want to live longer. I made peace with myself and my deprecators in my thirties. I try to live each day in harmony with all things around me. Does that mean I do that all the time? Of course not! But what I do is; clean it up as soon as I become aware of my mistake. That way, it leaves me unfettered and far more energetic because I can be at peace knowing that no lie will come back and haunt me in the future. Humans are on a learning curve. Regardless of who we are, we continue to evolve and learn. The person who harms others or steals does so because they do not know a different way. It is their environment and experience. We judge them differently. Imagine trying to teach a grade two student the basics of trigonometry. It can't be done (unless they fall into the Genius category). They must be taught gradually, with several failures throughout the process. We put murderers in jails to prevent them from harming others, but what if they just needed more time to learn? What if we taught them? People are not inherently bad, but we expect them to be at the same level of understanding as ourselves.

Some people tend towards laziness and don't conduct research for themselves, as witnessed by a former president in the U.S. who played loose with the facts. He took what was on social media and regurgitated them as facts, even though he had numerous experts on hand to provide accurate facts. As humans, we take many of our resources for granted. By ensuring we have precise and non-biased information at our fingertips, we can ensure our chances of success. Yet, we do not think twice about believing something on social media.

When my children were growing up, they used to ask me to give them answers to complex word problems. I could have easily given them the answers. However, they would not have learned about research, problem-solving, questioning, and weighing logic.

Another reason for falsehood may be their misguided confidence in their sources. Just because a friend told you that their friend told them a story doesn't make it true. Many people confuse opinions with facts, and that is because they express their views as though they are facts.

Finally, there is a danger when we don't know the entire picture. Let's say you have a coffee mug with different images on each side. The person across from you says, "I really like the dog on your mug." You look at your side and say, "That's no dog; it's a cat." Then you think, "What a dummy, they can't tell the difference between a cat and a dog." The truth is, neither has the complete picture. Both tell the world that the other person doesn't know the difference between dogs and cats. They provide examples. Of course, the conclusion drawn is based on a partial view, and is entirely wrong. Now, all those who had been apprised that this person can't tell the difference will say to their friends,

"This guy is an idiot; he can't tell the difference between a dog and a cat." And they will quote their friend as proof. Both will go on in their lives thinking that they were the one who was right. But in fact, neither of them were even close. This will happen when one person will not accept another person's version as possible.

XIII
PEACE OF MIND

Someone once asked me if peace of mind stems from happiness. The answer? It depends on what is causing the lack of peace in the first place. If we don't allow the circumstances of our lives to dictate how we feel, then the peace of mind and happiness are congruent. However, it is possible to have peace of mind without being happy. If our circumstances are such that things are going pretty much according to plan, you have few worries. But how you feel within yourself is up to you. You can decide that your day will be filled with joy, regardless of the circumstances, or you can choose misery.

To be at peace, we must be aligned in all our actions. Being at peace happens when we are content with everything that happens. There are no outstanding "I should have" or "I must do." It is challenging to be at peace if relationships need to be fixed.

Who in their right mind would choose despondency? Well, we do. The next time you feel depressed, look to see who the common denominator is. We want to blame anger, happiness, or any other emotion on others, but the reality is that peace of mind can be easily attained by changing our attitude. No one consciously picks misery, but your mind will say, "This is going to be a tough day" or "God, it's Monday; it is going to be a crappy start to the week." This is how we pick misery.

Having emotions is part of the human experience. What we do with them is all that we control. For instance, being angry is something that is disdained in our society. Yet, the energy that anger produces can be transmuted. Use that energy to feed the marginalized or seek equal rights for all. That, too, brings inner peace. It is better than using anger to harm others emotionally or physically, which does not lead to inner peace.

Inner peace is not found. It is within us. We have to let go of our inner turmoil to find it. Joy is also within us. Peel away the onion-like layers of anxiety, and the more layers that are peeled away, the closer you come to finding peace. To use another analogy, finding inner peace is like finding the calmness of an ocean. Waves on an ocean can reach 7 meters high, yet the further underneath the surface we go, the calmer the turbulence becomes. With people, the deeper they look inside, the quieter things become.

2

HEALTH

Health is the greatest gift, contentment the greatest wealth, faithfulness the best relationship.

Buddha

Sometimes, when things don't go our way, the outcome is far less important than how we react when our expectations are unmet.

When you're struck with illness, allow yourself to heal. The body can handle all manners of dis-ease. Our biological response is to get rid of the sickness as fast as possible. Our mental response is to pump ourselves full of different drugs and vitamins to become healthy rapidly. This course of action is due to our desire to alleviate and avoid all forms of pain and suffering-please; do not think that this is about anti-vaccination; it most certainly is not. This chapter pertains to the special group of people who rush to the doctor for every minute and minor illness, which could be biologically rectified if they had waited it out!

This is more about avoiding displeasure or not feeling one-hundred percent. It has nothing to do with Smallpox, Measles, COVID, and other debilitating illnesses that may cause infection or death to oneself or others.

Our bodies are designed to last for a long time. The eating of fast foods, fried foods, alcohol, drugs and other pollutants to our body shortens that lifespan. We fail to see what the long-term consequences are. Sometimes, we can't even see the short-term ones.

As we are younger, our bodies tolerate quite a bit. We lack awareness of how our body reacts to what we put into it. As we grow older, the food eaten becomes the norm. If we are athletic, we may not notice much difference in our bodies. But when we look at linemen in football who are way over three-hundred pounds, you can be assured it is not sustainable.

We suffer from diabetes at a relatively young age. We have a cure for that: insulin. The problem doesn't start there, it usually starts with what you subject your body to. I am not talking about those who are predisposed to it, but those who load up on things that your body simply cannot process.

The biggest problem is perception. We perceive that we are okay. No harm, no foul. Let's take a bag of sugar as an example. You remove a grain of sugar. The bag of sugar has changed, but you can't detect it. You may even take out a few spoonful's before you perceive a difference. Your body is like that bag of sugar. Each day, you give it a bit more to deal with. One day, you may wake up and notice your medicine cabinet is full of various medications to keep you going. And then you die. Well, we all die eventually. The trick is to live all of your life with joy and good health. This can be done by paying attention to what you put in your body.

Then there are things you may not have control over. Of course, you do have control over smoking, and that is another issue. When I was a child, I only knew one person who had Asthma. Today, there are thousands of cases- two in my family alone. My doctor also had asthma. A dear friend of ours recently passed away from Chronic Obstructive Pulmonary Disease. He worked in a glass manufacturing plant. In those days, they didn't know that airborne particles could cause that. My mother-in-law never smoked either, yet she lived in a house with smokers. My brother-in-law also suffers from breathing issues, but it was because he kept birds. There are fungi and parasites lurking in birds, creating lung disease in humans. I grew up in a steel town with a haze over the city, and I smoked. I was 38 when I quit smoking, but the damage was already done. Coming back from the clean air of the Himalayas, I noticed that my breathing was laboured. In fact, through the entire trek, I was labouring. I had put it down to altitude. I never acclimatized though; it was only when I returned that my doctor identified it.

Climate change, the industrial revolution and pesticides all had/have a negative impact on our bodies. And then we keep adding garbage to it. No wonder our lives expire early.

Recently, I was in a restaurant and observed a relatively young obese lady ordering a mixture of french fries and gravy. It was a large order. With that was a can of pop. I don't know if she had medical issues besides the weight, but these things are not independent of each other. There can be thyroid-related issues, but those people generally are mindful of what they put into their bodies.

We are arrogant enough to believe that we have a better plan than Mother Nature or science, which results in us trying to fix the natural order of things as fast as possible. We fill our bodies with drugs to suppress our innate healing abilities. We need a doctor to tell us if things will heal with drugs. We must ask our doctors if we can heal without drugs; let the body heal naturally. If not, allow yourself to take the necessary medicines.

That brings me to Naturopaths: I have seen friends that go there and swear by them. I digress; I have also heard of people walking away with hundreds of dollars worth of "medication" for a cure or prevention.

Why are we constantly being offered the "magic pill?" Some will say, "because it works." Fair enough. Except, may be side effects. Some can be severe. Have you ever seen some of the commercials the pharmaceutical companies put out? The list of side effects is so long you have to question why you would ever consider the drug.

Furthermore, there are side effects that will affect your immune system. If you think of your immune system as a highly-trained army that is ready to respond at a nanosecond's notice; why keep them locked up in their barracks while others fight for you? (in this case, drugs)

Over time, that 'army' will become lazy, stop responding or forget how to fight. Those are some of the side effects. But do we really believe that consuming vitamins replaces a proper meal or sunshine? I've heard the arguments about the importance of taking medicine. Yet, research tells us that most are ineffective or less effective than eating the proper foods.

As a result, we consume pharmaceuticals to live longer. Has anyone asked the question, "Longer than what?" I have not heard about someone never dying. We all do. What are we hanging on to? It's probably the notion that we have squandered most of our lives and hope to make it up in the stretch run. In our race to artificially achieve longevity of our lifespan, we decrease our life without knowing it!

You can be the healthiest person on the planet, and tomorrow you could go out on the street, get shot, get run over by a bus, step on an IED in countries that have buried them along the roadside, or perhaps you could get attacked by an animal. Life can be quite capricious.

Having said that, if you are healthy, you can enjoy life with fewer restrictions. The solution is not to tell the government (they can minimize the risk) to make things safer but to accept that we will all die at some point. We don't know when. So, as cliché as it sounds, live your days like every single one is your last! Love, forgive, apologize— make things right, tell the people you care about how much you love them, pick something you like to do and do it well!

Then, you don't need to worry about dying. Go off on another adventure.

I have come to the realization that, as a society, we worry too much. The stress of simply seeing one's medical reports can sometimes cause more medical problems to sprout. Concerning oneself with how long they will live seems sort of silly when you really think about it. There are so many clues around us that we simply don't know.

Some will argue and point out that people are living much longer than our previous generations. Yes, we have increased our lifespan, but at the individual level, who knows? I hear about more people having dementia. Is this an outcome of living longer? In earlier years, before medicine became much more sophisticated, we really didn't have a clue as to what was causing us to die early. There were many unknown deaths that we now have a clearer understanding of. Of course, wars also impacted longevity, but most advances in medicine have kept us away from the grim reaper for longer periods.

3

ENLIGHTENMENT

Before enlightenment, chopping wood and carrying water. After enlightenment, chopping wood and carrying water.

Zen Proverb

I
WHAT IS IT?

This Zen proverb tells me that there is no difference in how our daily tasks change between being enlightened and not being enlightened.

There are so many books on enlightenment, and people always talk about them as though it is accurate. Everyone thinks, "once I am enlightened, then everything will be different, and I can be above the fray."

Enlightenment is our ego's illusion, and the ego itself is an illusion of our mind. Eventually, people seeking enlightenment find a series of experiences that others consider enlightening. These are thoughts or experiences we share, and they differ from those that experience life differently. However, we are doing exactly what we were raised to do; it is only our mind that interferes with our progression. We are thankless: we look at life with a pessimistic view: we ponder upon what we do not have. This results in us overlooking the positive things in our life; we proceed to overlook all our natural abilities as well.

A fellow I once met in India's Kullu Valley was walking through a mountainous range with a dog. He was Swedish but had lived in India for several years. He taught Tai Chi up and down the coast. Our guide, who knew this individual well, asked about the dog; he met the dog on the trail, and the dog has followed him since. Then, he said something that struck me and has been with me ever since. He said, "Morty's (he decided to call him that) enlightened but doesn't know it yet." It struck me because this is precisely the same with humans; there is no difference. I even commented on that fact, "Oh, just like humans."

All who seek "enlightenment" eventually discover that it has been there all along. For instance, as Wayne Dyer once said, "why take a bus to Detroit when you are already in Detroit? It is the same with finding "yourself" and "enlightenment."

Unfortunately, the word "enlightenment" has lost much of its meaning, as it seems more like a goal to attain. When it becomes a goal, enlightenment is no different from becoming the next CEO or a professional athlete. Real knowledge is not like that. There is no endgame. A question, in various forms, amounts to "What is the fastest way towards enlightenment?" There is no fast way. There is no quick way of cooking a meal. If you turn up the heat, you will burn the food. "What is the best meditation?" That depends on you. You have to decide what works for you. Sometimes, the best for one person is not the same for others. "How do I get better?" Better than what? Better than yourself? There is no better. You are the best better there is. Does a peach tree look at an apple tree and ask itself if it can be better?

Enlightenment is not achieved by pursuing it anymore than a flower looks to the earth for its origins. This is your natural state. Our mind is there to convince us otherwise. That is why it is good to ignore it sometimes. In the process of trying to attain enlightenment, we go after so redundant things, yet here we are. Meditation can't get us there, despite what everyone says. There are some effortless ways of living. They include if you want to stop smoking, STOP! I am aware that many of you that smoke say it's not that simple. Start by taking a cigarette and be mindful of how it tastes, enters your longs and te pleasure you get from it. See yourself as a non-smoker. At the end of the excuses, it really becomes that simple. The key is intention. You must want it so much that you will forgo the cravings. Evolve yourself as a human.

Do you want to lose weight; well- stop eating so much! Eat a diet that differs from the one you have! I digress- it is not so simple, but you have to do what it takes! Consume less, exercise more. We're always looking for a quick fix. "Give me a diet pill so I can lose weight." The "Weight Loss" industry is a multi-billion-dollar business. I have seen several people join different dieting plans; they lose weight, only to regain it soon after. This is because those people don't want to change their lifestyles. They think it is like school; once you graduate, that is it. No, that is merely the beginning. Losing weight is not the endpoint. When we talk about enlightenment, people think the same way about wanting to lose weight; when I get the right formula, I will lose weight. When I am enlightened, I will be wonderful. I have a few hours. Can you teach me enlightenment? Sure, go into a dark room and light a candle.

II
GOING THROUGH THE PROCESS

We must go through the process. Whether that process takes us to visit a Zen temple in Japan (or San Francisco), a trek through the Himalayas or contemplation of our life on a bus.

Insights are readily available and come from the collective consciousness. Like a radio; you must be able to dial the right frequency to hear it. Similarly, you cannot hear the radio when your television is blasting, but the frequency is always there. You just have to shut or silence the television (mind), so you can listen.

When religion talks of one God, they really talk about one consciousness. Everything else is taught from books. Books cannot explain consciousness any more than we can. It is like trying to explain your feelings. We give them labels, so everyone knows what we are talking about. However, there is a whole subtext of fear, anger and joy that is inexplicable. And, if you could, they would be made up of words that point to the experience.

A lot has been written about achieving "enlightenment." The truth is that there is no such thing as enlightenment. It is a concocted word which describes an experiential event that happens to an individual and changes their state of mind. It is like trying to explain the in-between moment of not riding a bicycle to the realization that you are riding. In other words, it is indescribable. You can read all the books you want on how to ride a bike, yet you will not be able to ride unless you experience it. It takes experiencing balance and movement at the same time. It doesn't mean you can't pinpoint when it happens. I call this the "Aha moment."

People that tell you they are enlightened, by the very nature of what they are saying, are not. "Enlightened" people do not brag. There is a saying:

"Those who speak don't know. And those who know, don't speak." - Lao Tsu

In other words, you cannot explain or label the inexplicable. So if one does, it is a falsehood. Thus, the saying.

So, you will not become enlightened through meditation. That doesn't mean that meditation is pointless, but it will not enlighten you. It will allow you to silence the mind and tap into a universal consciousness. I haven't met too many "enlightened" people (it's a judgment), but I know of quite a few. One such person was Suzuki Roshi, a Zen practitioner and teacher. He died in 1971 at the tender age of 67 after founding the first Zen Buddhist monastery outside Asia, particularly in the United States. He even wrote a book on Zen and Buddhism called *Zen Mind, Beginner's Mind*, which was released in 1970.

We all die; I have not heard of a case where someone died of good health. There may be such people, I just haven't heard of any. Many self-help gurus in their forties claim all manner of things that work for longevity, but realistically, they haven't reached an age where some physical difficulties start setting in. They speak as if they know it all, but honestly, they do not know! Perhaps they listened to others, read health books, or quoted studies, sort of like spiritual leaders who can quote from the bible yet do not have any spiritual experiences of what they teach. We really are nothing more than sophisticated machinery with artificial intelligence. Much like cars that can drive themselves, we eventually break down, regardless of how well our "car" has been maintained.

We will all die; that is an unarguable fact: no matter how hard we try in vain to avoid the truth. The only thing we achieve by using medicine is prolong our time indefinitely, reducing the quality of the time we have left, as well as the time we gain by using such external chemicals. Instead, we can improve our longevity with a counter-intuitive approach where we simply focus on living and let our lives take their natural course.

I manage pain well. By studying our pain and its qualities and then understanding it, I have found that it quickly dissipates. However, sometimes the pain can be so acute that I forget to manage it. I am a person in my mid-seventies and always joked with my doctor that he would go broke if all his patients were like me. Having said that, I do realize that I am no longer in my prime. I have certain physical limitations, despite going to the gym daily. To think that we will (or should) remain as we were at 25 is merely the voice of our ego.

Of course, we do what we must to push back to continue enjoying those things we want to keep doing. I may not be able to climb mountains anymore, but I can still hike nature's trails.

With all that said, healing myself is the least of my worries. I allow my immune system to take care of itself through the natural course of action. That doesn't mean that I don't go to a doctor: if I need to go to the doctor, I do. Most of the time, I just eat what I like, and I am not hung up on the type of food I eat. I do care for the treatment of animals, and some farmers humanely care for their animals. I chose to eat vegetarian because meat takes a long time to digest and takes energy away from the body.

Life is beautiful, and we should enjoy it to the maximum. However, we should know that we will physically die eventually. It is not a state of mind; it is how the universe operates. Imagine if we all lived to be 150 or 200. The earth would be unsustainable.

III
THE END

Some people on spiritual journeys agree that enlightenment is an illusion and that it does not exist in reality. I take it a step further and concur that it is ego-driven. There is no endpoint to human evolution. To think that having reached Christ-like bliss or awareness completely misses the point. The spiritual journey has no endpoint. It is like saying, 'once you finish school, you are done with learning.' Schooling provides the tools to learn. The reality is that your consumption of knowledge is just starting. Once you get to where you think you are "enlightened" and play around with those feelings for a while; you too will learn that it was just a bench to sit on during a lifelong journey.

I have seen what I called enlightenment and had a similar experience. I have gone a long way past thinking that I reached enlightenment over forty years ago. To be enlightened about a subject also doesn't mean you have mastered that subject. So why do we think being "enlightened" about life is an endpoint?

The danger in harbouring the thought that you have reached "enlightenment" is that you may stop seeking. Some who have attained a peak experience sell it to others with the promise of enlightenment. Let us give those who think they have reached "enlightenment" a few more years and see what they think.

IV
ACCEPTANCE

I have come to the realization that the world did not go to hell in a handbasket; but that it was perfectly balanced. It took me a lifetime to get my head around this. There is so much negativity around us, that one would be disposed to think the world is tilted. However, looking at it from another perspective, there may be weighty environmental issues that many people are working on solutions for.

There is much unrest in this world. People are starving and displaced, yet many people are working on solutions. Religions have challenges, and many church leaders work together, regardless of denomination. Being interested in other people's views on life experiences will make us better-rounded humans.

After my experience with "enlightenment," I found that I was at a loss for several months. I felt I knew how the world worked and what my purpose in it was. So, there was nothing else to do. Even so, there was a lot that I yearned for.

For instance, why did I still think I needed more? I felt I needed more money. I was still managing my anger issues. Most of all, my relationship with my wife was getting shakier by the week. A truly "enlightened" person would not be chasing all these issues. So, what was it?

Gradually, I started to understand that what I was so desperate to seek was not outside of myself. I did not need to get on another bus heading for where I already was. I slowly began to accept things as they were and not change them or somehow wish they were different. I now take responsibility for my own life and not everyone else's. I started to understand that self-discovery was a journey with no endpoint. Some people are under the illusion that enlightenment is the endpoint-it is not.

Those who have experienced such things know there is always more. This is why I love the quote at the beginning of this chapter so much: it reminds us that enlightenment does not come from becoming enlightened and staying there. Enlightenment comes from remaining in a mental state of mind where we are enlightened regardless of how we are, where we are, who we are with, and what we are doing. We must accept that the universe wants things to be this way and carry on, despite what joy or sorrow the present moment may bring.

V

WHY WE FORGET

Forgetting is built into our DNA so we can continue to experience being human. One of the things I discovered on my journey was precisely that. I thought I understood how the universe worked and operated in that space of awareness for a while; I thought that I could create or bring my intentions to reality. Then I forgot; I had other things that occupied my mind. There are family obligations, work demands, and finances to be sorted out; the list goes on endlessly.

These are all distractions. However, they are also necessary traits of being human and operating in this realm. We still have the memories, but the experience has faded into the background. Being clustered could undoubtedly prolong the perception, but then we are not mastering being human.

Suddenly, an event or thought comes along, and the experience catapults itself back into our life. For instance, when all is in alignment, elevators open for us with the correct floor assigned, even though there is no one in the elevator. A parking space suddenly appears right in front of the building we wanted to enter, even though there wasn't a parking spot within a kilometre only a second ago.

How about when you are running late, and every traffic light turns green? Those are the times when enlightenment seems simple. When we forget, none of these things happen. We become frustrated because we remember what was available to us in our memory bank. "Why are my finances not in order? Why am I arguing with the family? I'm supposed to be "enlightened."

What we may have forgotten is how to enter that space again. The harder we try, the further we get from our ability to create. We create things all the time. And we forget it, but we are manifesting. Forgetting comes about because we fail to move with the flow of the universe; instead, we demand it to be how we want it to be. When we fail to remember, we see a wall and curse it for being in our way rather than stopping and looking for the opening.

There is a philosophy that says, you chose to be born into the life you have. Others, of course, will argue and say it is nonsense. Who cares, you are here and now. Regardless of whether you liked your parents or not, whether you didn't ask to be born, accept the fact that you are here, and what are you going to do about experiencing your humanity?

4

TAKING OWNERSHIP

By becoming self-aware, you gain ownership of reality; in becoming real, you become the master of both inner and outer life.

Deepak Chopra

I

FEELINGS

Taking ownership of your deeds and emotions can be a freeing aspect of the stresses we feel in life. For instance, having someone rudely talk to you can be very distressing.

As a result, we need to take ownership of that distress. When we say, "You hurt my feelings," you say that someone else is responsible for your emotions. How is that logical? Your feelings are yours.

When we discuss being disrespected, what we are saying is that I have no self-respect and need you to provide it to me. Some marry because they believe that they are in love. The significant other makes them feel good. The sex was fantastic, so that must be love. You seek others who will provide you with what you are lacking: love. Because you cannot give what you don't have, the relationship will always be one way. It should be okay to love someone, even if they don't love you. Sometimes we look for the echo effect. That is, you say, "I love you," and you wait to hear, "I love you too."

Requiring someone to be a certain way means you lack in that something. Thus, you are not taking ownership of your lack. That is why I love the above quote from Deepak. You cannot take ownership without knowing how you react to things. Why do you insist on your partner being a trophy? Because you lack something and need to accumulate things that will give you bragging rights. You need the approval of others. Since you already have your partner, you no longer seek their endorsement.

However, did you ever really need their endorsement? Did you ever really need their recognition? I believe not. Human beings begin to feel happier when they base their happiness on self-projecting themselves rather than the views or opinions of other people, no matter how special they might be in their life.

II
SEEING THE WORLD THROUGH YOUR VISION

I try to see the world as it is, not as it should be. I have realized that the world is in perfect balance. I don't have to do anything to rectify that. Sometimes, we are too singular and linear in our perspective on life, which is why we can't see the larger picture!

There are roughly 3 million people in Toronto, and of those, maybe one hundred pass away due to tragic circumstances. Does this mean that the universe is unbalanced? Is Toronto an awful destination? We see small "injustices" and jump to these types of conclusions:

"My God, what is happening? God must be mad at us; therefore, 'He/She' unleashes all these disasters or famines."

Our parents also taught us these things through their own upbringing and ignorance. If this is the intelligence we gather, is it not possible that computers can also collect false premises?

To clarify, by no means do I wish to whitewash these calamities. They should be dealt with. If one percent of the population dies from unacceptable circumstances, it may not seem like much statistically. However, if you are part of that one percent, then it is tragic.

Besides, how many other family members and friends are also affected? To do nothing to prevent or solve these problems is akin to standing in the middle of a busy highway, saying:

"God will protect me, so I have nothing to worry about."

Of course, you have something to worry about. We will constantly be in a state of flux. When one issue has been resolved, another one will arise to take its place.

The world will go on with me and will not without me. The world is truly a reflection of who I am. It's the same for each of us. We witness and see things from our point of view. We do not accept them as they are, but we judge them and make them the source of our disdain. Hence, seeking awareness or enlightenment is different for each of us. But the truth is universal. That truth has nothing to do with "my" truth or "your" truth."

You don't need to be the one who sees nothing but calamity, hate, anger, death, and destruction. Seek out those that are doing it right. Look for love, calm, people making a difference through charitable work. These are the circumstances that balance out the world. You look at the world and it determines your mood and feelings.

III
CHOOSE YOUR LEGACY

What do you want the world, strangers, friends or family to remember you by? I had a good friend who once asked me what I wanted my legacy to be at my place of work. I thought about that and how I wanted to be remembered in life. I concluded that I wanted people to feel better about themselves after interacting with me. We all have talents and skills; we should evaluate them and then offer them to the world.

There are so many signs and so many possibilities on this journey of life. We have a multitude of things to choose from. I can choose to be a spiritual leader or a pimp. (I'm not talking about the predatory type in this discussion.) It is all about how we wish to express ourselves on our journey.

We vilify and scandalize someone living off of the proceeds of prostitution, but is it any different from asking for alms from those people who listen to our spiritual messages?

In the old days, paying the church guaranteed a place in heaven; the peasant saved his pitiful, meagre alms to gain a place in that 'heaven.'

If the pimp (business agent) is in business with the unforced support of the prostitute and the customer, which one is wrong? There can be no perpetrators in life without victims and vice versa. We see victims as people we should feel sorry for. They need our assistance, not our feelings of sorrow. That just energizes both the victim and the perpetrator. Tell me when you are ready to move on from victimhood, and you can be helped. While you are in a state of victimization, it is hard to be supported.

As an aid, my mother used to help a woman whose husband was abusive. My mother gave her much advice about moving out, but for some reason, the woman never took the advice. I am not a psychiatrist and thus do not know why women stay in those relationships. Some people find comfort in being a victim until they get fed up with it.

This is not because they enjoy being tortured or beaten up, but because they either cannot leave something behind due to their actions or they simply do not know better. There are millions of people who believe that the state they were born in is destined to stay the same. Evolution is a part of life, and evolving your own life requires stepping out of your comfort zone. Take a look at the people who became exponentially rich: some never came from a rich family, but a rich family sprung out from them. It was because they strived towards changing their circumstances in life, rather than accepting their current predicament as 'God's will' or 'nature' etc.

Of course, there are several other factors that contribute to a person choosing to stop victimizing themselves and rising up to their real potential. It all eventually comes down to how they want to live out the rest of their life.

IV
LONELINESS VS. BEING ALONE

Do you answer "lonely" when answering the question, "How are you doing?" or are you fine simply being alone? Loneliness is associated with someone who dislikes being in their own company—being alone means that you choose to embrace solitude. Many times, that is by choice.

I have a friend who lived alone for many years and enjoyed a rich and rewarding life. Eventually, she met someone, but it didn't come from desperation and loneliness. They came together, not needing anything other than the chance to enjoy each other's company.

I am happily married, yet I enjoy being alone for periods of time. I get up two hours before my wife to be with myself. I enjoy working and spending time with my wife, and we make sure that there is time for us each day.

Before going to bed, I enjoy reading and relaxing. As selfish as it sounds, I relish the time that I dedicate to myself. That is not to say that I don't appreciate company; in fact, the opposite is true.

There are many lonely people in the world. Drinking does not solve the issue, nor do short-lived relationships; they are only momentary relapses from loneliness.

We really need to look deep within ourselves and find out why we don't like to sit with ourselves and why we need to rely on others to love us and make us happy.

V

Awareness

You cannot take ownership of something if you don't know that you are doing anything. That is why I placed "awareness" at the beginning of this book. I guess there are no dumb questions; I used to think that was the case until I started to ask what some consider to be stupid questions; it was because I didn't know any better.

It is the same with others. I was somewhat amazed at the naïveté of questions posed by some, which I now understand and recognize as a younger version of myself. Besides, when we say questions are dumb, we form judgments.

I know some people who hate liars, yet I find them at certain points also lying. Does that not tell you that they hate and lie themselves? We all lie; it is a big deal, not because of judgemental reasons, but because our lives work better when living with integrity. I worked with someone who wanted to fire people the moment they "screwed up." You can't effectively manage people like that because they start lying to avoid punishment. It becomes the parent/child syndrome. A stern parent will admonish a child, and the child learns to lie to avoid penalties. This conditioning manifests itself at work and elsewhere in one's life. We make commitments that we have no intention of fulfilling.

I agree to be somewhere for 5:00 PM, and I show up at 5:10 PM. However, if my flight leaves at 5:00 PM, I will be at the airport by 3:00 PM because I don't want to miss my flight. I am indicating to the person I was to meet at 5:00 that they are not as important as what I am currently doing. Thus, arriving at 5:10 can be easily justified. Priorities define what you want in life and what you are willing to work for. There is no such thing as being busy all the time. If you often repeat this mantra to your family or friends, or if someone does it to you, then don't run away from the reality of human nature. If you prioritize them, you will make time for it. When you don't prioritize, you come up with excuses like the one mentioned above.

This essentially restricts your flow of energy. Your personal integrity is out. It's difficult to mend problematic situations if you cannot be honest about things. We should also realize that being honest does not give us the right to pass judgment; there is a marked difference between both actions. Commenting on someone's race, sexuality, gender or religion is also a lie. We don't know everyone or what they believe in. There is much more than the surface level. You must be patient and open to concisely comprehend the waves in which they exist. You can only add your two cents to a discussion or an argument.

Even then, it would not be a universal fact, just your opinion. So, the question is, how can we possibly say that a group of "bad" actors represent an entire species? One sour fruit does not define the entire produce.

Imagine this: If I landed on this planet out of the blue and the first thing I saw was a person beating up an elderly person, I would harbour the assumption that it would be dangerous to be an elderly person in this society. I would presume that all the young people are thugs and cutthroats. However, that wouldn't make my assumption true. That is how many of us react, and it has nothing to do with the truth. Truth has many faces and every person carries a different so-called 'truth.'

VI
ETHICS VS. CONDUCT

Each of us has skills and abilities that others don't have, or to a greater or lesser degree. Instead of emulating those skills, we wastefully squander them to try and mirror other people's strengths.

True wisdom is derived from experience; it has little to do with learning- even though learning is an element that may point you to a specific direction.

Alan Watts was a great student of Zen Buddhism. He had some personal demons; nonetheless, I still consider him much more aware of the universe than I am.

We put our spiritual leaders on a pedestal and expect them to live up to our morals. Why? After all, all spiritual leaders are also human. I grew up in the Eastern Orthodox religion and my father had many friends, including priests and bishops. Over the years, some would visit us at our house.

As they did not have to "perform," I saw their essence as human beings. That is not to say that they were rowdy or bad behind the curtain. No, it is to highlight that they would have regular conversations and share anonymous anecdotes of parishioners and priests. All in all, they were human beings first.

I greatly admired another person's teachings on exploring myself to a deeper understanding of who I was. He was also a womanizer; this was not the most outstanding attribute to have, especially considering that he was a spiritual leader. However, he made a difference in many people's lives, including mine.

Then there is someone many may be familiar with: his name is Werner Erhard. He made a difference in so many people's lives and continues to do so with his coaching; he was also accused of being a terrible husband and father.

There are a couple of points to analyze from this. Firstly, we should not place our moral judgments on others; the law takes care of that, and if not, the universe does. The second point is that we all have something within us that makes a difference, regardless of other issues.

As long as there is an incongruity within us (our outward expressions not matching our inner beingness), we will continue to be in turmoil. When we become consistent in our inner being and outer actions, we legitimately become energized.

Be the person you show the world to be. If there is a distortion between the two sides, then you will exude a sense of distortion. You need to be in perfect harmony with what you represent and what you are in reality.

The world is like a masquerade party with masquerading figures looming here and there in utter confusion. You have to break out of the loop and step not only for the ones around you but for yourself. Our environment radiates with influence. Use it to defeat the turmoil bubbling in every being.

5

MEDITATION

Meditation is not a thing. It is not doingness but beingness. There is nothing to do. Just be mindful, aware and non-judgemental.

Arno Ilic

I

IS THERE A RIGHT WAY?

We all experience different things, and there are literally hundreds of methods. Stay cautious of the self-proclaimed gurus who say that their methods are the only correct way to meditate. These 'gurus,' 'yogis,' 'spiritual men.' etc. then charge a fee or "donation." There are quacks in many different professions.

The beauty of meditation is that it is a very personalized experience. Just how your experience of being human is your perspicacity, so too is meditation. There is no point in comparing experiences unless you think something is wrong. We read a lot and hear a lot about what to do, what not to do, and what meditation will do for us.

There are those that, not in so many words, want to "fix you up" by having you meditate. They are trenched in the belief that there is something wrong with you – the fact is, there isn't. It is another piece of programming you have that you have either come to accept or bought into the idea itself. If you really want to meditate just because there are some things you may wish to consider.

Meditation may or may not let you discover how many ways you are like a machine or computer programmed incorrectly. Meditation allows you to be with yourself for the amount of time you give yourself. It can be for an hour or so; even a few minutes, perhaps. Remaining in your own company can be scary for some people; they avoid being alone by staying busy and using drugs or alcohol to numb their senses. Self-journeying is a tricky yet meticulous process. Consider it to be a process of untying a knot. Two things can take place when you are at it: One, you can either unwind the knot and discover something you are looking for. Or two, when you open the knot, you might get intimidated when the knot unwinds and there is nothing to see.

II
BENEFITS OF MEDITATING

Meditate for the sake of meditating. I have been asked what you get out of meditating. I don't have a direct answer to that question. I have read about altering brain waves, becoming enlightened, mindful, at peace, and all sorts of other things that you can think of. They may all be true for some. Some just seem to answer any of the above without really knowing what these things exactly mean. You see, personally, I don't know.

I meditate because someone once said that it would bring you mindfulness. So, I meditated. I have also done several other things besides meditation. Which ones had the most effect on me? I don't really know. We are no longer the person we were at the age of ten. We think differently, act and react differently, and we are physically different.

What do you attribute that to? Probably more programming. We can say meditation changed us, and it probably did to some degree, but in which way and how is still up in the air for me. So now, and for the past decades, I meditate because there is no other explanation. I do not meditate to gain anything. When you have everything, there is nothing to attain.

III
GETTING STARTED

Meditation is one of the most effortless, yet challenging things to do. The reason it is easy is that there really is nothing to do. The hard part is letting your mind's thoughts go by and simply bringing awareness to them. Some people say that they meditate to get enlightened; there really is no such thing; it is most likely the ego talking. After all, if you are enlightened, you have separated yourself from the masses. There is a heap of ego in those thoughts.

There is no specific time to meditate. I used to meditate twice a day, morning and evening. Now, I meditate once a day for a little longer, mainly in the morning. I have meditated at different times during the day to ensure that I complete my meditation time. I used to meditate right after getting up in the morning and found out that sometimes, I would fall asleep during the process.

I now meditate after shaving and taking a shower. I may even have breakfast – I might read the newspaper, all before starting my meditation. The beauty of meditating is that there really is no right time or the right place. It is probably not best to meditate after eating, as it may slow your metabolism. Someone also suggested that it may not be suitable to meditate following a run or heavy exercise. I'm not sure, as I am much more alert after exercising.

Having said that, I have meditated in the early hours of the morning for the past few years without falling asleep. You know yourself better. Figure out what works for you and then work accordingly. Don't rush the process.

When meditating, sit somewhere where you will not be disturbed for the next 20–30 minutes. You can sit in a chair or cross-legged on the floor or cushion; it doesn't matter. Become aware of your breathing: you can focus on it initially by counting to ten. Count out odd numbers as you inhale and even numbers as you exhale, or you can exhale on the odd numbers and inhale on even numbers, whatever works for you.

If you find yourself thinking of something else, gently go back to the beginning of your count. Don't change your breathing; the purpose is not necessarily to get to 10. The objective is only to observe, and even that isn't quite correct, as there is no purpose involved in the process of meditation.

If you are a novice, you may want to count to 10 on your breathing and then repeat. Do not get discouraged if you don't reach ten. You may encounter thoughts that comment on breathing quality, including when you get close to ten or are frustrated that you can't get to ten—each time you notice that- simply start over.

If you have lost your place, no problem, start over. The "goal" is not to get to ten; it is merely a direction. As in life, we veer off the path from time to time. When we realize we have strayed, we return to the road again. Repetition doesn't exhibit failure, but success in the form of steps conquered.

You can meditate with your eyes open or closed. Anyone can meditate on their own. Are there any risks? Perhaps there are, but there is a risk in anything we do. That shouldn't stop us. Besides, you will know what is right for you and what isn't. Meditation is a singular experience. Don't be afraid to take a leap.

Once you are comfortable, stay in that position for 20 minutes to start; don't move. Try not to scratch an itch; just let it be. Notice your reaction to wanting to scratch. If you are sitting cross-legged, you may sense an ache in your legs. Just notice that and then let go of the pain the same way you would let go of thoughts. You may become aware that you judge, but let that go and start counting again.

You have to steer yourself toward a comatose mind. At first, it won't be easy, but it is achievable. Your thoughts will keep wiping you away like an ocean wave. Do you remain in the fallen position when it strikes?

No.

You stand up and wait for another wave to come. After a while, you get used to the pressure hitting your body, and you overcome it. Likewise, overcome your thoughts and park your mind in the peace lane.

I kept glancing at my watch for the first few months, wondering when the time would be up. I would procrastinate a lot and try to prevent thoughts from emerging- until I realized that they would be there regardless. Then, I just let them go.

Initially, I saw interesting visions, and I wanted to recreate them. I understood that trying to repeat a meditation was not really meditating. Then, I recognized that the images I saw were simply illusions.

I continued because I wanted to meditate. I didn't have an end game. It was just something that I wanted to do. Gradually, 20 minutes became 25 minutes, then 30, and now it is inching towards 35 minutes per sitting.

A painfully restless mind when meditating is not unusual for a beginner. The beginner will eventually discover a less hectic psyche without the input of those who want to "help."

IV
EXPERIENCE

Feeling good has nothing to do with meditation. Try finding happiness and joy in everything you do. Meditation is a great way to spend time with yourself, but it is not about feeling better.

Feeling bad is a mindset. Perhaps you may discover why you don't feel good in meditation or professional analysis. I wake up feeling good, and I go to bed feeling good. It is something that I cultivated long before I started meditating. I don't allow the circumstances in my life to dictate my feelings. The best thing is to let go of how you think or feel.

Understand who you are, and start enjoying the little things in your life. Observe the things that annoy you and try to figure out why that is the case. From my experience, annoyance is never because of the other person or thing. It is always you (me). We chose to be sad, annoyed, angry and so on. These things have very little to do with meditation.

When we argue with our spouse, friends or colleagues, the common denominator is always **you** (me). We tend to give situations and people power over ourselves. What you feel starts with you. Your body is like a car: the steering wheel is your reaction. Who the driver is; impacts the ride.

Don't be fooled by how others react to meditation. In some instances, the effects of meditation can take many years before you notice the changes. Each one of us has different experiences. Take a half-full glass of water, and take an eyedropper of water. Add a drop at a time. How many drops will it take before you notice a change? Observing changes is similar to monitoring changes within yourself. Meditating is subtle. Know that just because a person's viewpoint works for them does not mean that it will work for everyone in the same manner. You are a different human being. We all are different.

Over the years, I discovered that there is no "correct" way of meditating. There are hundreds of different techniques, and you should explore alternative methods of meditation to find which one suits you best.

When starting, you might feel good or see "spiritual" things; do not judge those illusions. Simply accept them and don't look forward to repeating the same experience the next time. It is all about awareness. The more you become aware of your thoughts, feelings, and emotions, the more you will choose how you react to circumstances.

You may experience some remarkable things while meditating, but that is not the objective. After practicing for a while, you will realize that those are all illusions. That's fine. The thing about meditation is to let things simply float past. When people talk about emptying the mind, some interpret it literally. The reality is that you simply let thoughts flow or drift without holding onto them.

It frees you and allows you to be the observer. Then you can ask who the observer is. After all, the mind cannot observe itself any more than you will see your eyeballs. In the darkness, you will figure out who the observer is.

V

THE RIGHT WAY TO MEDITATE

I have been questioned about the right way to meditate. There are different ways and disciplines for meditation. There are books on meditation, and then there are various sects and religions that also teach you meditative techniques. Choose one that resonates with you. The following story illustrates how helpful people can derail your own experiences.

A monk meditated in the forest; a bright light emanated through the woods and could be seen for several kilometres. One day, an abbot was walking through the woods. He was attracted by the light, and he thought that he should investigate. When he came upon the monk, he noted that he was in meditation.

When the monk stopped, the abbot asked him what mantra he was using for his meditation. The monk told him, and the abbot said, "No, no, that's wrong. You should be using this mantra," and he gave him the one used at the monastery.

The monk thanked him for the correction. When the abbot departed, the monk began to meditate with the new mantra. The abbot walked away, pleased that he was able to help a young monk, the brightness in the forest slowly started to diminish.

Even an experienced "helper" must let others find their path. There certainly is no "correct" way to meditate. At times, we feel that we are doing others a favour by helping them, but we are not. Processes like meditation are personal activities. Everyone experiences it differently. It is not a textbook lesson that all can follow and agree to. It requires personal effort and an understanding of what works out for you.

VI
MISCONCEPTIONS

There is no goal for meditating. Annihilating the mind is a silly concept. The more you try to get rid of the mind, the greater the power your thoughts have over you. Many people try to do this and get frustrated because they can't destroy the mind. Trying not to think when you are thinking is impossible.

Similarly, what is emptying the mind? Do you have a garbage disposal or an empty drawer into which you can dump your mind? That is not the goal. It can happen naturally, but it is impossible to do if you **try** to empty your mind. The reason being that the harder you try, the more you fill your mind with thoughts about purging it and why it is not working. Once you become conscious, it erupts, so you have to do the opposite, you have to let it be.

We think we need to meditate to become better people. That is another misconception. Meditate because **YOU** want to, not because you think you will become a better person or, worse yet, become enlightened. You are trying to live up to other people's standards rather than being you. Do this effort for yourself.

What measurements do you live by? How do you wish to present yourself to the rest of the world? Even criminals have a code of conduct they go by. Meditation will not change who you are. You have to do that yourself. Meditating may show you what you are doing, so you can be more aware of reacting or judging situations or interactions. After that, it is up to you to make the necessary adjustments in your life. Like everything else, meditation is not a magic pill. Stop looking for one and start doing the work it will take to make your life work the way you want it to. It won't solve your problems; only you can do that. Don't depend on external motivations to improve something in your life. It is an internal process.

The essence of who we are does not change. How we express ourselves or our behaviour can change. Those things change based on programming from external sources. What meditation allows a person is to experience oneself without the internal dialogue telling us how good or bad we are. Meditation tends to create gaps in thinking over time. That is when we truly see ourselves. That self does not need changing. Perhaps that is why I talk about the external influences that affect the "outer" me when I say I don't know if meditation has changed me. In other words, the way I communicate with people and the beliefs I carry come from external influences that shape my behaviour.

Compassion, love and joy come from within. Meditation may help you get in touch with them.

Some people meditate because they think their self-esteem will improve or they will be more confident; they will be shrewder, better at love, have a clearer mind and just a better way of being. In other words, all their problems will disappear.

That's not what meditation is about. What you are asking for are qualities that you have within yourself. You generate happiness from within and bring it to all you do. Bring your joy to meditation. Don't expect meditating to give you pleasure. Bring your self-esteem and confidence into meditation; don't look for it there. You become happier if you become grateful for all you already have. Stop wanting what you don't have and start appreciating what you do have. Find happiness there. Bring joy to all you have, not your disappointments of what you don't have. Gain confidence in doing that which you lack confidence in.

Confidence isn't something that you wish for, and it appears.

Your life will also become much more apparent when you stop wishing for things you have not and are not. A maple tree does not desire to become an oak tree. Figure out who you are.

Meditation is not about doing something. Just observe. Some time ago, I had restless leg syndrome, which would manifest when meditating. Initially, I would resist it, thinking it took away from my meditation. As a matter of fact, it was part of my meditation. Once I let go and accepted the restless leg as a friend, I invited it to be part of my meditation; it started dissipating. I have not had that issue for many years now. If you leave your mind alone, it will be fine. There is no up or down in energy, by the way. It is neither; it just **is**. It sits in the realm of the non-physical, thus neither here nor there or up or down.

Hoping to avoid the uncomfortableness of socializing and hoping that meditation may help you do that is living a lot in "hope." Unfortunately, hope does not move the needle. The action moves you from hope to a result. Be with uncomfortableness; let it wash over you. Perhaps meditation can, over many years, help with that. However, you may still feel uncomfortable. That will not go away by meditating. Embrace the discomfort; go ahead and start a conversation.

I used to be quite shy. I had an acquaintance who encouraged me to start conversations in an elevator. We were in Detroit at the time, taking the elevator to our office. He commented to me in a voice that everyone could hear, "Do you ever notice how no one talks on the elevator?" That started everyone in the elevator laughing. Now I regularly talk to people on the elevator. I can't tell you how uncomfortable it was at the outset. Now I talk to complete strangers. But it requires a willingness to do so and breaking through our fears.

If that doesn't work, I suggest seeking professional help.

VII
DEPRESSION

Meditation is something between you and yourself. I am by no means a psychologist or psychiatrist, but when I get depressed, I choose to be depressed. Some people I know try to fight depression (that which you resist, persists.), causing more problems. Now, I am not talking about clinical depression, which needs to be seen by a professional, but ordinary depression should be acknowledged.

I don't mean to say, go ahead and wallow in it, but admit it and get on with what you are doing. You may also wish to explore where exactly in your body depression simmers. What colour do you see it as? What were you doing just before you became depressed? How long is it if you were to take a ruler and measure your depression? How deep is it? How wide is it? What are the physical sensations?

When you do that, you may find that the feelings become diminished; if you do it several times, they may even disappear. Failing that, meditate with your depression, but don't expect meditation to clear up your depression.

VIII
HAPPINESS

Meditation does not create a sense of joy any more than someone complimenting you. No, joy and happiness come from within. I find it is a waste of time to feel bad. I always think it is a mindset. Try bringing happiness and joy to everything you do. Meditation is a great way to spend time with yourself, but it is not about feeling better; it is about observation. Perhaps you might even discover why you don't feel tranquillized during meditation or professional analysis. Why not wake up feeling good, and go to bed feeling elated? It was an attitude that was cultivated long before I even began to meditate.

Do not allow the circumstances in your life to influence your mood; the best thing to do is understand who you are and start enjoying the little things in life. Observe the things that annoy you and try to figure out why. Annoyance is never about the other person or thing. It is always you (us). We chose to be sad, annoyed, angry, and so on. These things have very little to do with meditation. When we argue with our spouse, friends, or colleagues, the common denominator is always you (us). Being disgruntled comes from expecting a particular behaviour or outcome of others that fit within your belief system.

IX
NOTICING CHANGES

It is impossible for me to relay the changes meditation has made in my life. I am sure that there have been many. The difficulty is in identifying them. I read a lot, take seminars and interact with many different people. Since meditation happens in a subtle way, it is hard to identify. Many things I have read and discussed with people have given me pause and had me look at things from a different perspective.

Besides, it doesn't matter. How we get to where we are today is determined by us. We do not always accept 100 percent of everything we are told or read. This is because we are not what we are told or what we read. If you read this book in its entirety and conclude that 90 percent is nonsense, that's okay too. That means that 10 percent of this book and its contents have resonated with you.

There are two things that I can attribute to meditation. I still do much other work, including Zen studies, and I am a voracious reader, so many different knowledge sources are at play. I can attribute a greater sense of awareness within. In other words, I am getting better at not reacting to outside stimuli and diminishing the urge to say something.

The second thing I noticed is that I tend to stay more 'in the moment' than ever. Mind you- I have been meditating for close to 30 years, so changes are subtle.

So, if things don't happen right away, be patient. I did not start meditating for a reason or to get somewhere. Then, one day, I looked around and noticed those changes within me. I still have difficulty assessing if they came about through a particular event, discipline or whether they would happen just in the process of living life.

To illustrate the point, imagine buying a large tub of honey. The first few times it is used, you see no difference in the amount used. This may happen for several days. One day, you look and realize that the jar has been noticeably depleted. The same analogy applies towards meditation. The only difference is we are talking about years, not days.

Either way, enjoy meditation just because. And, you can also relax because you will turn out exactly how you are supposed to. You can look at plants for a point of reference. Some produce beautiful flowers, others are just coloured leaves- some are poisonous. They are what they are. No amount of wishing they could be different will change that.

Humans have one remarkably different ability: the ability to formulate an opinion. This causes stress. You don't see plants ever stressing over the physical attributions of another or observing the 'evil' persona of a poisonous plant. This is because they do not possess the ability to comprehend these concepts. What is, is it for them.

If there is something that stresses them out is the lack of necessities, not superficial or self-made scenarios.

X
JUDGING MEDITATION

I don't judge. Negative or positive effects are the same; they are a result or outcome; we add the negative or positive. Perceiving them as one or the other means that we should only have "positive" meditational experiences. When meditating, only observe. Once you get past the notion of "good" or "bad" meditations, you might start to notice that you experience other things in negative or positive terms.

For someone to say they are not very good at meditation is a judgment on their part. It means that in their mind, certain things should or should not happen when they meditate. They think that meditation is about calming your mind, when it really isn't. (It can be an outcome.).

It is more about the observation of the mind. The problem is that there is so much false information, probably from those that tried it. Meditation is not about emptying the mind; it is not about being calm; it is about sitting with yourself and observing.

Observe that you are "not doing well" with it. Recognize when you have thoughts about school, finances, relationships, and whatever comes to your awareness. Those are all a given. Remember that you are there to meditate; let those thoughts pass.

When using a mantra, gently repeat it whenever you notice yourself thinking. Applying a counting technique can also be fruitful. Count to ten, odd numbers as you inhale and even numbers as you exhale. When you have reached ten, start over. When you become aware of a thought or lose track, start over. Notice if you get frustrated if you can't get to ten. It doesn't matter! Go back to counting.

I have been meditating for 30 years and still cannot reach 10 at times. My thoughts have become way more subtle than they used to be. Don't worry if you are doing it right or wrong. It does not matter. What matters is that you are doing it and observing how you think the sounds around you, the smells that surround you, and how you react to them. When you become aware of these things, do not start thinking about them, but gently let go of what you notice and go back to counting.

Years ago, when I started out, I used to be at peace after meditating, only to become argumentative when I returned to my daily routine. That only started to dissipate once I let go of the thought that I shouldn't be in a contentious state following my meditation. It is all about letting go. This is what is meant by non-attachment.

People were always under the illusion that it meant non-attachment to objects or money. While that is also true, you shouldn't be attached to their ideas, philosophies, or beliefs. You can have all of them, including currency and priceless objects; just don't let them become appendages.

Some people find aspects of meditation disturbing. What struck me was the question, "how do I avoid disturbing thoughts? When talking about "avoiding," red flags should come up. Why are you trying to avoid anything during meditation? Incorporate whatever "disturbances" into your meditation—minimize distractions. When my children were young, I told them that there would be no interruptions for the next thirty minutes unless there was a fire and certainly no arguments during that time. That minimized the chances of being so disturbed that I would have to stop my meditation dealing with minor situations.

When I had fallen asleep and was unable to meditate in the early hours of the day, I would meditate on the commuter train to work.

The commute to work was a forty-five-minute ride, so I would start meditating as soon as I boarded. There were plenty of distractions that came about: people trying to find their seats, having compelling conversations beside and across from me, the constant stopping and starting to load and unload passengers. Even the announcements for the next stop could be distracting.

The key I learned from this was twofold.

First, I would not allow these distractions to deter me from meditating.

Second, I would incorporate the noise and ambiance into my meditation. This was a little trick that I learned from the late Wayne Dyer; he mentioned that he meditated on the lawn of the Hawaii hotel he was staying in. There was a person with a lawnmower, cutting the grass around him. It was a noisy distraction; however, he had learned to incorporate this into his meditation.

As a result, my suggestion is to keep meditating, note the distractions, and continue meditating. I came to a realization that one of the biggest distractions was my mind: I kept ruminating. I initially thought that I was not supposed to think. I naively thought that meditation was to have an empty mind. That turned out to be false. Notice how when you are thinking, you can not think – you **are** thinking. The trick is to let go of your thoughts. In other words, have a focal point that you can return to. It could be a mantra, focusing on your breathing or counting. You may also get agitated because you can't finish counting to ten without having thoughts. That's okay. Counting to ten shouldn't be a goal; it should be a direction. Note what's going through your head and start counting again. The more you notice, the more you will see; thoughts get subtler as you go. Don't let that distract you.

The key to meditation is that there is no endgame. In other words, when you meditate, don't have expectations. Just observe.

What gets stale about meditation? Anything can get stale after a while, including movies having similar storylines or plots. The taste of food can also get tiresome. When things get old, marvel as though it is the first time. Don't judge your meditation as being worn. You considered it as such. When eating an apple, eat with mindfulness. Look at the polished smoothness of the apple, the colour, and then take a bite. Taste the sweetness or tartness of the apple and the texture. Check out the core and see how the pips are nested within. Look at the smoothness of the dark pips, then taste the apple. That way, the taste never gets old, nor does the apple. Each apple is unique. Other fruits and vegetables have the same aspect. They are kind of like human beings, unique in their own way.

The next time you sit down to meditate, do it as though you have never done it before. Be in awe of everything that comes up for you. Of course, you will have thoughts. Notice the thoughts that pass you by, the ones you analyze; along with the ones that take you completely away from your meditation- just because you thought of a math equation, and just wanted to get the answer before returning to your meditation. How important was that? Imagine driving down a road lined with trees. You are aware of the trees, but you think no more of them. Suddenly, you come across a grand oak tree or a red maple tree. You say 'wow' and continue to think of its beauty for some time. That may remind you of yet another thought which led to the reminiscence of another beauty, perhaps your partner. Then you think about the argument you got into with them this morning. Did you notice how far your thoughts have taken you away from simply driving?

That is sort of how meditation also works. You may have several ideas that go by, and there is no reaction. Then, something grabs your attention, you start thinking about that and the thought perhaps leads you to another. When you do notice this, it's no big deal; just go back to meditating.

Wow! I didn't have a single thought. Oops, there is another thought. I need to stop thinking while I'm meditating (good luck with that)

Enjoy the experience, and if you can't, ask yourself why. Maybe you just got tired of your own company. Perhaps you are stale. Enthralling thoughts that perhaps now can be answered. Good luck.

Sitting and doing nothing for 20 to 30 minutes is the most extensive challenge: I kept looking at my watch to see when the time was up. Then it went to all the thoughts I would have. Gradually, I let go of all that and just be.

It is normal to overthink, from what I have witnessed. Many people do so. In the end, it can cause stress. Meditation can help or hinder that underlying stress. If one tends to overthink, it may manifest in the meditative practice, leading to more frustration. Learn to focus on one thing during meditation; when observing your thoughts, gently fixate on your focal points such as breathing, a mantra, your body, or a word that was decided on. The key is to always stay focused on the present. It may be a long road, but slowly, we learn to focus 'in the moment' in time. *"The Power of Now,"* a book by Eckhart Tolle, provides excellent insight into being in the moment.

Before starting your meditation, I suggest counting odd numbers on the in-breath and exhaling on even numbers. If you find yourself thinking, just start over. Things may come up, such as, "this is easy." "I'm almost there," and a myriad of other thoughts. Not to worry, just start over. Notice if you get frustrated, then carry on.

XI
ILLUSIONS

When in a state of deep meditation, it is a good idea to come out slowly and adjust to the surroundings. In meditation, hallucinations or a form of ignis fatuus can sometimes be controlled by analyzing them. For example, what colour, how big, and what form they take, etc. The more you study them, the lesser they become until they disappear.

The more you are worried and fearful of them, the more they will hang around. It is somewhat unusual to have "hallucinations." There are, for sure, things that happen during meditation and bring incredible effects. Some people get so attracted to them that they think this is what meditation should be.

Meditation is about observing without drawing any conclusions. Fearing hallucinations is fearing an illusion. Sometimes, it is easier to get professional help, especially if one cannot get rid of them.

Seeing lights is part of the same meditative state as feeling super calm or losing focus. They are all one. When you ask about focusing on your breath longer, you are already in a state of doingness. Meditation is about not doing, only observing. Concentrating on your breath is also doingness, although it is generally a good starting point for beginners. Awareness is not doing. It is also what carries no thoughts, no actions, and no judgment. So, I would suggest continuing to meditate and observe your reactions until you reach a state of awareness.

I have a different take on meditation. I have been at it since 1993; I am a relative novice. Over the years, I have found that the technique one uses should be based on what works best for the individual. It is silly to suggest that there is only one way to meditate.

One would think that there is an endgame to meditation. There is not, from what I have experienced. I would like to meet someone that claims to have entirely quietened the mind. What meditation allows us to see is our thoughts without evaluating them. It enables us to see how judgemental we can be.

You may even have cogitations at the beginning of, **am I doing this right?** *I'm not getting anything out of this! I'm wasting my time; thoughts flow into my mind of* **important or exciting ideas**. That, too, becomes a judgment for great ideas, which are only thoughts. It is us that makes them "great," i.e., judgemental.

Finally, beware of those who claim their way is the only authentic way. It is not, but who is to say that it doesn't have relevance or cannot resonate with you?

Wishing to be wealthy and prosperous is an illusion in the first place. Meditation or any other type of spiritual path will not get you there. It is not the mentality that lacks, but that you have a "lack" mentality that keeps you from many things such as love, respect, money, etc. You might change your perception of what your view on being successful or rich is.

If you have access to a computer, that puts you ahead of many on the planet. You are already wealthy and successful. The only thing that is getting in your way is your ego of wanting to be like the rich and famous, who, may I remind you, have issues of their own.

We tend to look at them as role models for being that way. The reality is that the only one we should compare ourselves with is us. If I were to compare myself to, say, Donald Trump, who is affluent and privileged in the eyes of many (he held the highest office in America), then I would be considered a failure. I have neither his position nor his money.

I have a wonderful family; the children are well-educated and have their own families. That, to me, is successful. I have a beautiful wife of 39 years. I am blessed with grandchildren, and every day that I wake, I am full of joy and surrounded by beauty. That is my definition of success. I don't have the money or riches of others. It is not that I don't desire certain things, it is just that I recognize those desires for what they are; they are ego-driven. In my mind, I simply say thanks for sharing, and go back to focusing on what I was doing.

When trekking through the Himalayas, I met families who had to walk miles to procure firewood for cooking; they lived above the tree line. Their eyes had joy and happiness, despite not having a television or radio. Or, perhaps, because they didn't have those amenities.

Their children did not have fancy sneakers or the latest fashions. They did not need them to be rich in experiences and successful because they had a yurt and some sheep. Wealth and success are in the eyes of the beholder: it is a concept, and a perspective. For some, it is never enough. For others, happiness comes from what they have, no matter what their station in life is.

XII
EXPECTATIONS

Do you have expectations around meditation? One shouldn't be looking for anything from meditation; meditating is a very personal experience. You cannot compare what one person experiences with another's- that is the beauty of meditation.

If one has already concluded an expected outcome, it may not appear to work for you. It is working; you simply don't know it.

I have seen questions from people wanting to know how to recreate certain experiences. Sometimes they see things they perceive to be cool. What to get out of that experience is to realize what your judgment says is cool, and is an illusion because all you are left with is the memory, and we know that isn't real.

Beyond that, if you meditate to recreate that experience, it is no longer meditation. When I was a child, I had an intense dream, but it was interrupted when the alarm went off. I was so focused on the outcome that I actually continued the dream the next night. The outcome was inconclusive, and I realized it was a dream that had no value other than coming to that very conclusion.

XIII
LETTING GO

I usually throw a basketball at the hoop and miss getting it in. When I was a pitcher, I did not always throw strikes. I just rededicated my practice and got better. The same rule applies to meditation. Rededicate your ability to let go.

Being anxious does not allow you to let go. Hence, try to stop being anxious. When you feel compelled to hold on to a particular point of view and notice yourself doing that, let go.

Perhaps bring your mindfulness to breathing or another part of your body. When I first started focusing on my breathing,, I started having difficulty breathing. My instinct was to alter it. That screwed up everything. I began bringing my attention to just counting from 1 to 10. After a while, I noticed that I could become aware of my breathing without altering it.

What I am saying is that you are on the right path. Be patient; leave your expectations of how you should do things behind. Continue doing what you do - let the natural order of things take its time. I never played professional baseball, but that didn't deter me from playing or loving the game. It's the same with meditation. I'm sure plenty of people practice meditation whilst thinking their method is superior. That is not the case; this is not an intellectual classroom. Sometimes there are no correct answers: It's what works for you.

Meditation is not an exercise. If you want to exercise, go to the gym. If you wish for some mental activity, do some problem-solving exercises. Mindfulness is to do nothing. If you become aware of a slight breeze, you are just cognisant; you don't need to do anything with that information. The same holds true with meditation.

In everything, nothing can exist. In nothingness, nothing exists, including everything. Physics tells us that energy cannot be destroyed, it can only be transformed. Therefore, there is no such thing as nothingness; it's only a concept to explain a lack of something. In reality, there is always something we may not be aware of, which doesn't mean there is nothing.

XIV
AWARE VS. OBSERVING

When you are questioning if you are in your mind, you are. You seem to think you can be "out of your mind" while meditating. There is a difference between observing and being aware. Observing is a level of doingness. Being au courant does not require anything; there is no action required at all. When you "observe," you are already judging.

We cannot observe without thinking something about what we are observing. As you meditate, check out the difference between being aware and observing. Are you observing because someone suggested that you do so?

Over the years, I have heard so many different opinions on meditation; some of the ideas are pure nonsense - coming from individuals who have no direct experience but have read a book or a friend told them about it.

A student once asked Shunryu Suzuki if he could explain Buddhism in a nutshell. He thought about it for a minute, then said,

"Everything changes."

And because everything changes, what is written eventually becomes a lie, including my observations. In reality, you are on your own journey, and all I can do is point you in a direction. You will come to your personal level of meditation.

You see, the mere act of meditation requires nothing. There are no goals to reach. You don't need to feel better, or worse after meditation. You may experience calmness or not. In other words, meditate for no reason. Observe if you like. That, too, is a process in itself. From the time I wake up to the time I go to bed- and for as long as I can remember, I start by enjoying each moment of the day. The same routine applies to meditation.

Sit in a quiet place without distractions. (Later, you will be able to meditate anywhere). If there is one, the purpose of meditation is to get to know yourself better; that is, try to watch what is happening around within you without judging or trying to change anything.

Many people that meditate start by observing their breath. When you bring your awareness to breathing, you may also notice that you are trying to change your breathing or breathing consciously. Just notice that.

Another way of meditating is to count your breaths going in (odd numbers) and breathing out (even numbers) or count in reverse order. When you have reached ten, start over.

If you catch yourself thinking, or you lose count - start over. The purpose of doing so is to have a focal point when you notice that you are contemplating or pondering. Gently go back to either counting or observing your breathing. That is meditation in its raw form.

Of course, there are far more sophisticated practices that charge money, but the reality is, you don't need that. Lastly, I would say that there is no wrong way to do this.

In the seventies, I experimented with hallucinogenic drugs to get a more profound sense of awareness. While it altered my perception and was fascinating, I also knew that if drugs could do this, so could I; it opened me up to many things I could do without drugs.

Meditation is somewhat similar: While we look for innermost experiences, they too, are an illusion, like drugs and alcohol. The same can be true of becoming addicted to these feelings.

We should be looking at why this is important to us. However, in our meditative state, we should do no more than just be aware, then let go of that awareness, just as you do with many thoughts.

Years ago, I attended a seminar, and one of the things they talked about were three different types of learning: visual, auditory and kinesthetic. The seminar leader indicated that visual attainment was superior because it was the one that most leaders identify with. Then auditory and, finally, those who were highly emotional were most likely kinesthetic learners.

An overly excited salesperson came up to me after the break, announced that he was a visual learner and concluded that I was probably a kinesthetic learner. I thanked him but thought that this was an individual who wanted to learn simply to be better than someone else.

I was more amused than insulted. What difference does it make in how we absorb information, so long as we do? The seminar showed me different learning forms, and I discovered that I learn best with visual and kinesthetic.

I am constantly reminded of this because learning, like anything else, can be double-sided. One can learn to help, and one can learn to hold it over others. Meditating to get a "deeper" experience indicates a desire to be superior instead of simply meditating.

Zen Buddhists talk about doing a task; they do not talk about doing it better, but about doing it by paying attention to 'doing'—nothing else. The same goes for meditation: just meditate and pay attention.

No need to evaluate or try to get deeper. That also evokes the question, *"Deeper than what?"* If it is deeper, does that mean there is going to be an endpoint or a bottom? I have been meditating for 30 years- and have yet to find a base. But then again, I haven't been looking for one.

When you observe without intent, you don't worry about 'doing'; you are aware.

XV
ATTACHMENT

Back in the late seventies, a lady talked about thoughts. She gave an example by using a tissue and floating it along. She described it as clouds just drifting along. We have hundreds of ideas we may be unaware of that are similar to that floating tissue paper or "clouds drifting along." The lady then sucked the tissue paper in as it floated past her mouth. That, she claimed, was what happens when we suddenly make these thoughts worthy of our attention as well as our subsequent judgment.

When you meditate, let them go. I found the most effective way to let go is to go back to what you were doing. For instance, if you meditate with a mantra, gently go back to the mantra. If your focus is on breathing, gently return to that.

In the end, life is hugely effortless if we let it. Otherwise, we make life complicated. Some even blame their difficult life on others or their circumstances. We determine how complex or straightforward our life is.

XVI
DISTRACTIONS

Hearing your heartbeat while being aware of breathing is an awareness of both. Everything can be a distraction if you pay too much attention to it. That being said, there can be a difference between "awareness" and hearing; you just need to be mindful of it and return to your point of focus.

At some point, you should also stop using noise-cancelling headphones because you need to learn to be aware of the sound around you without having it become a distraction.

It is difficult to advance your spirituality by trying to eliminate distractions or unpleasantness. Having been sequestered for a lifetime in a monastery, some monks have difficulty when they leave.

They must deal with and understand the day-to-day living issues amongst people who do not walk their spiritual path. There is noise pollution, environmental pollution, harassment of people, and several things not associated with monastic life. That is not to say it does not happen, but the scale is different.

It is way better to accept things the way they are rather than resist them. Resistance causes persistence- you don't need to prevent noise and distractions. Let them become part of your meditation.

Perhaps when you get to the point of letting them go, you can shift your focus from breathing to nothingness. Creation comes from the void; you become aware of yourself and how you created your universe. Behind nothingness exists everything, allowing you to create.

There are a couple of things that I noticed when I first started. The first was trying to get it right and failing miserably because there is no "right;" that is why we need to let go of doing it right. The second thing is letting go of judging experiences by thinking they are "good" or "bad" or "wow;" this must have a great deal of meaning'.

There are some other things to look at as well. Some people think that meditation is about clearing the mind of all thoughts. It simply is impossible, and those people have not meditated for long.

Yes, you can have glimpses of nothing, but as soon as that happens, you will notice, thinking, "Hey, I have no thoughts." The mind just seems to work that way. I also recommend having a focus when you start meditating. That way, when you notice your mind wandering, you have something to return to. Through all this, you may see you are distracted from being aware.

Remember: there is no end. Think of it as a walk-through of nature. You don't go into a forest expecting an outcome. However, you will have many thoughts and experiences as you walk through the woods. Just observe and observe your judgments. Then go back to counting.

Problems arise when you try to stop thinking. Meditation is not about controlling the mind. Have you ever tried not thinking while you are thinking? In meditation, just let your thoughts flow.

Don't interact with them, and don't try to stop them; simply let them float past your mind like clouds drifting in the sky. Have you ever argued with yourself? It becomes pointless. The same applies to your thoughts: the more you try to control them, the more they will be with you. Once you learn to let go of them, you will begin to see tiny gaps of no thought. Those are the periods when you will notice a qualitative difference. It does not mean that that is what meditation is all about, or that somehow you can manipulate your thoughts into being quiet. It doesn't happen that way. Just sit and let your thoughts go.

Some meditation techniques use a mantra or observed breathing; they do this to continuously centre themselves. When you recognize that you are thinking, it is good to have something to return to - let your thoughts continue to travel without being stopped by your energy, giving your thoughts more power.

I have used a variety of different meditation techniques: I started with TM and have transitioned into several different ones; I currently use Zen meditation.

To suggest or ask that meditation can be rated on a scale is misguided. To say there must be success is to need an outcome. None of the ways I have meditated had to do with being "successful." Looking for success means looking for a result.

When we start meditating, we may see an array of things that we judge as awesome or pretty cool. As cool as they are, they are also a distraction. The next time we meditate, we expect to constantly see these kinds of things, yet they are just illusions.

When starting a subsequent meditation, question what is considered a "successful" outcome. What is the need to have a result? When having been at it for a while, notice that an outcome is something one cannot let go of.

While working, I have given up my pictures of what an outcome is. I have a goal and a process to reach that goal. Once the process is in place, I let go of the pictured target. You see, if we have a goal of, say making $1 million over the next five years, and you have a plan of getting there, do you stop because the goal has been reached? What if you don't reach your goal but become financially secure? Isn't that the real goal? If you are stuck with that picture of $1 million, then you may not feel "successful."

My advice is to enjoy the meditative journey just for the sake of the trip.

We tend to make our lives complicated for some reason. Life is relatively easy, and meditation is even easier. It's essentially sitting for 20 - 30 minutes without doing anything but breathing. Think about it, how difficult can that be?

Still, we find ways to make it difficult. We struggle with our minds.

"Is this the right way to meditate?"

"I'm bored."

"This can't be all there is to it."

"Am I breathing the right way?"

"Is my time up yet?"

"Yesterday, I felt like I was going into the light. How come I can't repeat that?"

"How do I find myself?"

All these questions and more, we ask ourselves. I can find dozens of reasons to complicate meditation. It really isn't: we need to stop trying to control the process of "getting it right." Getting it right is for exam papers. Meditation is not an exam.

All you are required to do in meditation is simply awareness. Observe your breath. Be aware of your thoughts, sounds, and smells. That's it. Don't judge any of it, nor engage in long thought processes about it. Otherwise, the rest are just distractions, as they are in day-to-day life.

XVII
OBSERVE

You may think you had an enlightening experience or an "aha" moment. So what? Just observe, don't judge. Don't try to repeat your experience. If you do so, you will not move forward and might frustrate yourself if your experience is not repeated. I would suggest finding a comfortable space to sit. There seems to be a matter of opinion on how you should sit, depending on the type of meditation you have learned. I have found little difference in where or how one meditates; the key is to sit in a relaxed position and do nothing.

Life is pretty simple if we keep it that way, meditation even simpler.

XVIII
BENEFITS

Why are you meditating? If you meditate because you think you should, perhaps you should quit. I started meditating 30 years ago; I started just because- there was no reason.

I still wonder what the benefit is because people tell me they have received so much from meditating. In all honesty, I don't know if the changes in my life happened from meditating or just the process of life itself.

Who cares?

I get a chance to sit in solitude and observe my thoughts- that's it. I never started meditating for a benefit. Perhaps this is because I started when I was older and already traversed down the path of self-awareness and total awareness, the interconnectivity of all life forms and energy in the universe.

So, when I meditated, I wasn't overly concerned about whether I was doing it right or what I would get out of it. As I said earlier, I don't know if the benefits of my life are a direct result of meditation or not. It seriously doesn't matter.

Here's the thing I noticed: life is incremental. One day, you wake up and realize you are no longer a boy or girl, but an adult. All the while, growing up, you may wonder when you can become a teenager or adult, and then voila! Here you are. All this time, you are anxious, but life doesn't care. You will either grow into adulthood or you will not. Being worried about growing up does not matter. Besides, the more we focus on this notion, the more frustrated we will get as seemingly, nothing happens.

Let's examine a bag of sugar: as we open it, we notice that the bag is full, perhaps weighing one kilogram. Now we remove a grain of the sugar. The bag looks the same, the amount of sugar. It may even weigh the same, but there has been a change that is imperceptible. So it is with meditation. Should we keep removing grains of sugar each day, perhaps in a few months you may perceive the change. It's the same with meditation, except it may take years before you notice a change, or if you are very perceptive, months.

A young man was working out in the gym. After each workout, he would go to the locker room and look in the mirror. I could see the disappointment on his face as seemingly nothing was changing. The reason: changes are incremental.

The point is that you won't see any difference in your life after meditating, perhaps for months or years. That doesn't mean nothing is happening.

Regardless, you should do it because you get to observe things about yourself. Continuing with meditation may reveal why you need to be rewarded for doing something. You may find out why you have to justify meditating, so you need to tell people that you are successful at it because you had some insight or other.

You cannot meditate to manifest money into your life! You have to change your poverty consciousness. Asking for more money tells the universe that you don't have any or not enough. In other words, you are lacking. The universe agrees with you. Long before having money, you have to be a person with currency. In other words, your mindset needs to be that of a wealthy person. That doesn't mean you go out spending money frivolously; it means you act and behave as a rich person does. Come from a place of prosperity, find abundance in everything—and live life with integrity.

We have the entire way of doing things in reverse; and then we wonder why things don't work. For instance, I need a lot of money to do good for others. Only then can I be the person I want to be (whatever that may be). This is entirely reversed from how things work. Many people follow the philosophy where they believe that they need to **have** money to _be_ rich; once they attain wealth, they can **do** something serviceable for society. They can assist at charitable events (You don't need money, and you are doing something). Take the focus off yourself and put it on others. Start in reverse order. Act as though you **have** abundance in your life; that you are already wealthy, therefore, you don't need anything. Now you get to **be** rich. Act as though you are; act how wealthy people act. You may not be rich at the end of the process, but you may find that you have become the person you wanted to be.

Don't follow what you see on television, those are just illusions of how the rich live. People that are "real" and wealthy do not flash their wealth. It is part of who they are; most wealthy people are highly philanthropic. Do you see how this is reversed? First have, then be, and finally, do.

We tend to think that money buys happiness; it does not. Authentic joy is derived from within and needs no money. Perhaps delve a bit deeper into what that money is going to do.

Look, people buy lottery tickets because they think this will buy them freedom and allow them to do all the things they can possibly dream of. Seventy percent of lottery winners are broke shortly after winning a few million dollars.

Why?

It's because they are poverty-conscious. It is also why it is nearly impossible for people on government assistance to get off it. We need to work on changing people's mentality towards lack.

I watched children at the foot of the Himalayan Mountain range who had very little but were very happy. They had less than some of America's poor people yet are far healthier mentally and physically.

As this chapter is about meditation, and I emphasize the importance of not having expectations, you may discover during meditating that you have a lack of something in your life. That may come as a thought, but that will not change anything. The knowledge of something does not change anything. It is what you do with that knowledge that will make the difference.

6

MANAGING THE BRAIN

Nothing is more precious than being in the present moment. Fully alive, fully aware.

Nhat Hanh

I

MIND GAMES

Much is written about being in the moment, including the best seller *"The Power of Now"* by Eckhard Tolle, *"You Are Here"* by Thich Nhat Hanh, and *"The Power of Moments"* by Chip and Dan Heath.

There is no reason to go into this at length because you can find much more descriptive books regarding it. Suffice it to say, when you are present at this moment, it is the gateway from chaos and survival to peace and tranquillity.

In other words, nothing else is going on with you. You are not concerned or bothered about your mortgage payment, overdue credit card bills, what to wear to this evening's dance, or what meals you need to prepare to keep everyone happy. That is because you are engaged in the present moment.

The mind tends to play tricks on us. Sometimes, it creates fantasies that are fugazi, and other times, it gets you thinking about the what ifs: what if you only had done this or accomplished that differently?

When you fantasize about not wanting to go to a party because you don't know anyone, it will probably become boring as you only know the host, who will be busy with their other guests. Of course, once you get to the party, you are introduced to many interesting people, and at the end of the night, you proclaim that you have had the best time ever. Mmm, why does the mind do that? I went to my niece's wedding and my brother introduced me to a number of people. Of course my brother, sister-in-law and niece were preoccupied, so I spent a great deal of time talking to people I did not know. It was both rewarding and enlightening.

Now you are restlessly talking about that great night you had many weeks later. You have mentioned the events of that night to anyone that is still listening to you. You can start questioning why the mind continues to go on about an experience that is no longer an experience, but only a fond memory.

I, too, have often wondered about the misdirection of the mind. In the present moment, there is no misdirection. So, what leaves the mind out of things in the present moment? It is because the mind is not real: it deals in probabilities, possibilities, doubt, and hubris- the mind provides the illusion that only outside sources can make you happy, sad, or angry.

I have concluded that all this misdirection is for us to look deeper into ourselves. Most of the things that we pursue are available from within. Do you want to be happy? Generate that from within yourself.

Do you want riches?

Perhaps you need to change your mindset from poverty consciousness to abundance. You may also discover that you don't need more. You already have everything you need.

Your mind longs for a ten-bedroom, ten-bathroom house with a four-car garage; despite the prospective inhabitants being only you and your wife. You want to have a better lawn than your neighbour. Your neighbour drives a Bentley, so you feel the need to have something equally good if not better. These thoughts are all driven by your mind.

Look, to put it simply: don't discount your brain altogether. Without your brain, you will not find your way home or even your car keys. The brain, for sure, serves a valuable function.

Consider your brain to be a mystery to be solved. Somewhere within you, a part observes the brain; if you listen closely, it can tell you what is true. You see a person of the opposite or same sex that you are physically attracted to. It does not mean that they feel the same way about you; it does not mean that you can touch them or do anything your mind wants or tells you to do.

A deeper knowing recognizes that it does not serve you to do something about your thoughts. It is what keeps us respecting both ourselves and the other person.

It may also keep us out of jail or keep us from losing a lot of money at casinos or races. Sometimes, people gamble by playing cards or roulette because it keeps them in the present moment. They are physically and mentally engaged.

However, there is a cheaper way of being in the moment: do something constructive such as volunteering your time. I guarantee, that in the long run, you will gain more satisfaction and be richer for the experience and your wallet.

7

FEAR

Our deepest fear is not that we are inadequate. Our deepest fear is that we are powerful beyond measure. It is our light, not our darkness, that most frightens us. *We ask ourselves, 'Who am I to be brilliant, gorgeous, talented, fabulous?' Actually, who are you not to be?* You are a child of God. Your playing small does not serve the world. There is nothing enlightened about *shrinking so that other people won't feel insecure* around you. We are all meant to shine, as children do. We were born to make manifest the glory of God that is *within us. It's not just in some of us; it's in everyone.* And as we let our own light shine, we unconsciously give other people permission to do the same. As we are liberated from our own fear, our presence automatically *liberates others."*

Marianne Williamson

I
THE ORIGIN OF FEAR

Fears manifest in several forms, such as unease, worry, anxiety, nervousness, tension, dread, phobia, etc.

Unease - usually associated with something that has not yet happened and may not. An example is the feelings the world has about North Korea's nuclear plans.

Worry - a condition caused by an event that has not occurred and may or may not, such as worrying about whether there is enough money to cover the rent or groceries this month.

Ego -The ego is not a thing but is part of the mind we ascribe to that which has us thinking we are better than others, we are not good enough, and some of those things that we attribute to the devil. The ego is never satisfied and will always want what you don't have and doesn't care about what you do have. Ego will allow you to feel good about taking advantage of someone (E.g., I managed to sell the car for $1000.00 more than the list price) and then later feel guilty that they did take advantage.

Nervous - a feeling usually associated with a fear of failure or an unreasonable expectation. People waiting to be interviewed for a job they feel is vital to them may experience nervousness.

Tension - tension may exist between two people who are afraid to voice or express their true feelings for fear of repercussion. A co-worker may be acting in a way that disturbs you, but you have a fear of telling them. However, keeping this bottled up inside will build tension between you and the co-worker.

Dread -this happens when you are concerned about another person's reaction to some "bad news" that you may have to deliver.

Phobia - a compulsive and persistent fear that may be carried over by traumatic events such as fear of high places, fear of death, fear of crowds, etc.

All these, you will notice, are manifestations of fear. Each event is only based on the mind and not in the reality of now. Because these fears only exist in the mind, the ego views itself as being constantly under threat. When that happens, a siege mentality takes place. As a result, you are constantly on the defensive. You worry about being overweight. Did you pay too much for that dress, that car? How do I look? Why is she/he looking at me like that? You constantly question yourself.

Fear has attached itself to the ego, so you now fear loss, getting hurt, and being wrong. It is the ego that worries about being wrong and sees it as a threat to its very existence. Since we fear death, being wrong is the closest thing to expressing one's demise. Why else do we have to be so entrenched in our point of view? This has such a strong pull on the human psyche that arguments have ensued, friends lost, and wars erupted.

Once you have freed yourself from the mind, you are no longer interested in keeping or maintaining a position. This is not to say that you don't have a point of view or belief, but you can state it firmly without being defensive or aggressive.

Be aware of defensiveness. What are people defending? It is most likely an illusion. It is ego-driven if you protect your honour, for you are already honourable and need no defending. You can bet if you catch yourself defending something, it is usually to safeguard a fear.

Your mind constantly seeks to escape. It can be uncomfortable in the present; your mind prefers to think about how it could have or should have been. Rarely does it remain in the present moment with what is so. The more you honour and observe the present, the more you free yourself from pain, suffering, and the ego mind.

If you remove time from the mind, you can stop it. You can only be trapped in time through the mind. Time is the compulsion to live through memory and anticipation; it is unwilling to honour the present. You live this way because the past gives you an identity, and the future promises salvation, hope, or fulfillment. This time is the most precious instant you have because it is really the only thing you have. 'Now' is also the only point from which you can free the mind.

When you live in the moment, you will start feeling aliveness. Nothing ever happens outside of the now. Whatever occurred 10 minutes or 10 seconds ago transpired in the present 10 minutes or 10 seconds ago and is no longer authentic at this point in time; it only exists in your mind – an illusion.

Foreboding comes from the unknown; that is natural; don't avoid it. Make fear your friend. When recognizing it, simply say thank you and put it in your pocket. As for the future, we must understand and acknowledge that we are not a predictor of the future. If you are, start betting on horse races and the stock market. The expectation is an illusion that we make up. There is only one place where the future exists, and that is in your mind. Once we understand that, we can start to let go of worrying about the future. If we have an accident that may result in bleeding or soreness, won't we forget all about the future? Suddenly our focus is on stopping the bleeding or dealing with the pain. There is no future because we are in the present. Once we experience this, we can slowly start letting go of our expectations. Living in the present moment allows us to experience much more peace and far less stress.

Something to think about

1.   Begin to notice your fears. Are you worrying? If so, what are you worrying about? Is there something you can do about this worry at this instant in time? Notice how you feel about that. Do you have any judgment about that? Can you let it go?

2.   Are you excited? Why? What comes up for you when you get excited? Are you excited about something happening right now, or did it pass? Are you excited about a future possibility? Observe your excitement. Where is it coming from? Why are you excited about an event that may not happen?

II
BEING IN THE MOMENT

One of the things you will notice with children is that they are in awe of everything. They experiment with their feelings. They do everything because it is usually their first time. We need to get back to that state as adults. We think that being childlike is to play games and not have a care in the world. Well, that is true, but that comes from a clear mind. Children, if you notice, live in the present moment. Adults live in the future and the past. They think about the wondrous things that happened or didn't happen. They think about mortgage payments, meeting deadlines, and where their next meal comes from.

There are two things we can do to get back to childlike fascination. The first is to see the world as you've never seen it before and start looking at things as though you have come across something for the first time. The second is to live in the present moment. These are hard things to do because we are so ingrained in our thoughts that everything is like everything else — except not always.

When you find yourself thinking about something in the past or the future, remind yourself of the present. Be fully engaged at this moment in time. When you walk by something, stop and look at it as though you have never seen it before. What is its colour? What is its texture? How large or small is it? Have you ever noticed how children like to touch things? They are learning different textures. When they touch that thousand dollar vase, we scream at them not to touch it instead of letting them touch it with our guidance. That is how you keep your childlike sense of wonder alive. You can also do this with the food you eat.

Overthinking is a habit. Hence, it can be broken. That's why it is a habit. Our "voila" and "aha" moments happen when there is a gap in our thinking. Once we have the "aha" moment, our mind starts thinking and analyzing. We can always break our "overthinking" habit by returning to our present moment. Note that most thinking happens either about the future or the past. Neither is real. Therefore, we are left with the only alternative: to stay mindful in the present moment.

For example, if you are worried about your next mortgage payment and/or that you may lose your house, you're worrying about something that is not in the present moment. If I grabbed your arm and cut off your hand, you would be in the present moment and no longer worry about the events in the future, i.e., your mortgage. Now, we don't have to go to such extremes, but you get the point. If you are not doing anything in this instance other than thinking, shift your awareness to your breathing. That will bring you back into the present moment. It is why we suggest bringing your attention to breathing when meditating. It keeps us in the moments of now.

Stress or anxiety comes mainly from thinking about everything other than what you are doing in the now. Failing to be present at this moment will cause a range of emotions, many not good. Someone once said that no matter what troubles or problems one has, they can disappear instantly. Whatever you do in this instance brings your full attention to that. You will live a much less stressful life.

It can be said that all things in the mind are illusions. The mind cannot possibly settle down with all those thoughts. By writing down your thoughts, studies, money, and the future don't exist. They are all illusions of the mind. A broken relationship is merely the universe telling us that the association no longer serves us. Again, the relationship is only in your mind. Let's say that after spending an hour preparing your food and plating it, you drop the entire thing on the floor. Guaranteed that we no longer worry about studies, past relationships, money, or other apprehensions. Now the focus is on real-time, cleaning up the mess and not looking to start all over. When you're focusing on the present, all your troubles go away. Worrying about the future is like a tomato seed, wondering if it will turn into a tomato. If we just live our life day-to-day without concern for the future, we will be fine. Relax; life will turn out exactly as it should. So, make a conscious decision to enjoy it. Bring joy to everything you do.

Like other mood-altering drugs, self-talk is used to avoid harsh realities. A person once suggested that if you desire to lose weight, stop eating. At the time, I was thinking of losing about 5 pounds. Gaining and losing weight is an outcome of how we eat (unless there is a medical condition). I saw what he meant. We tend to consume food mindlessly. Our stomach dictates when it wants to be fed, and we satisfy that craving without giving a second thought to what goes into our body. We may distract or even disassociate from the food we are eating. We eat many other things that cause us to demand more. The question arises, "who dictates your life, you or your mind?"

When we become mindful of our food, our concentration is 100%. We become familiar with the textures, colours, and tastes of each food item we consume. Then, when we combine these tastes, we experience different textures and flavours. Finally, we watch it go down to our stomachs. How does our stomach react to what we just put into our system? Does the brain feel sluggish? Do we need to sit down and just vegetate following that meal? I look at someone's plate of chicken wings. When I came to Canada, no one would eat chicken wings; butchers would routinely give them away. Chicken wings are unhealthy to begin with, and then we add high-calorie sauces on top of that. According to Nutrition Facts, twenty medium chicken wings provide a whopping 1840 calories (fatsecret.com). Now, try a treadmill at the gym and see how long it takes you to burn off those calories. We delude ourselves by saying there are no carbs, so we can eat as many as we want. If we don't burn the calories off, our body will store the rest as body fat.

We come to a choice we can freely make. Is this food supporting our highest self? Do the textures and colours please us? Of course, we cannot do this with a fast-food burger because we don't know what has gone into it. Some people who want to lose weight think it lies in their self-talk. They believe that that will change their attitude towards eating. Well, how has that worked? The truth is that we need to eat every spoonful or forkful with the most enjoyment possible. Instead of merely shoving it in our mouths, think about each spoonful. Put the fork down once there is a mouthful. Chew it until there is nothing left in the mouth before picking it up again.

III
PAST LIVES

For the most part, Karma is in our mind, similar to how we make up sins. We tend to look at things through time and space. Therefore, we assume that there is a past and a future. In reality, there is only now; the rest lies in our brains.

I recall sitting in a workshop in the '70s, and an aspect was to explore past lives. I deduced that the brain made up most of our past lives. It comes from what people wished they were. The vivid pictures come from memories based on books or visual images they may have seen in this lifetime. When you read a book about centuries past, you have a mental picture of what that era would look like. This is not unlike your thoughts about living in the past. Some people genuinely believe in their past lives, affecting their present life (Karma).

Research suggests that quarks, one of the fundamental building blocks of the universe, theorize they have memory. (A study from Dr. Hosein Nasrolahpour from the Department of Physics at Tarbiat University in Tehran, Iran).

When we die, our brain dies, as does the body. Since energy does not die, only transform, there is an element of us out there, but purely in energy form. Do electrons have memory? According to the study above, yes. Does it remember your house number, profession, or life partner? No, but it goes somewhere out there when it dissipates after dying. Karma may be part of that energy, but it doesn't remember that Bob did a bad thing in his past life, and therefore Elaine has to suffer the consequences of her past life. Quarks may have memory embedded in them, but it is more like muscle memory that is separate from the brain's prefrontal cortex.

A river does not retain memories of its previous destination; however, it does retain energy. Humans, on the other hand, keep memory in the brain. That comes from life experiences (another form of programming). If we somehow tap into the quarks of the universe, we think it is our consciousness. The molecules that form us are similar to the molecules that form snow. That is, snow in the winter dissipates into the water in warmer weather, providing vitality to the trees and grass. Does the nutrient the water offers plants remember that it was snow at some point? Likely not, as it is the same molecular structure in a different form.

Back to Karma and past lives, when the brain dies, memory dies with it. However, you may be able to tap into other sources and think they are yours. Therefore, when you believe you did something terrible in your past, you are paying for it now. Someone may have done something "bad," and it could be a portion of your memory that causes you to think it is you. To illustrate this further, if you are happy sitting in a room and another person enters, you notice your mood has suddenly shifted. This shift may not be due to you, but the other person's mood you picked up.

Presently, quarks are the smallest known energy particles out there. Some speculation is that quarks consist of preons, but that hasn't been proven yet, and we haven't developed instruments small enough to detect them. We may if we have the right frequency to listen and tap into that base. Just as we cannot hear radio waves without the proper receiver and the correct frequency, universal knowledge is also available. We speculate. Wise men and sages of the past didn't have current scientific studies to work with.

Sometimes we wonder why we have the thoughts we do. The answer, in a nutshell, is we don't know. When we have those flashes of past memories, realistically, who should care? Unless those memories are significant in your life and relate to unfinished issues, it shouldn't matter. If it is not life-changing, treat these memories like any other thoughts. In other words, looking for answers to why an event happens does not change the outcome. It may alter future events, but if you are not changing something or trying to prevent something, the whys don't matter.

Similarly, if you want to know why we turn out the way we do, and a professional tells you it is because you were beaten or neglected as a child, having that knowledge in itself will not change your behaviour. It only lets us understand why we behave that way; what is relevant is what we do to stop our unwanted behaviour. For the most part, this example is to say the "why" answers alone will not alter anything.

8

THOUGHTS

Right thinking comes with self-knowledge. Without understanding yourself, you have no basis for thought,

Jiddu Krishnamurti

I

PERCEPTIONS OF THE MIND

While thoughts are a constituent of awareness, they are also combined with perception. Thoughts seem to permeate every aspect of us, so I give them a chapter of their own.

Thoughts are like the memory in a computer. When computers were first programmed, there used to be an expression, "Garbage in, garbage out," or GIGO. Essentially, it meant that if you programmed the wrong thing in, you would not get the desired result.

Our brains follow the same pattern. We tend to think that our minds are intelligent, and that we are in charge of our thoughts. After all, a computer cannot possibly program itself. Well, that is not true anymore. Machine learning, a subset of artificial intelligence, can do precisely that. So, our minds are no different than a computer. It adjusts itself to new data. The problem is that we don't add virus protection. Essentially, humans are stimulus-response machines.

Hence, if someone tells you a plausible idea and you believe it to be real, you have created a virus within your brain, not a medical one, but a "computer" virus, and the question arises, "what are some of these viruses?"

Let's look at this historically. In the beginning, long before radios, books, televisions, or computers, there was only verbal communication. There were a few things to discuss, such as crops, weather, and ideas. Essentially, stress was derived from survival. That could have been farmers relying on the weather or hunters depending on finding food. Because these things tended to occupy the mind, it was usually easier to deal with the present. There were no books or movies, let alone the internet, to distract them from what was possible. They may wonder about rain for tomorrow or if the game will be available the next day. In other words, they tended to live much closer to the moment. Once religion was brought into the equation, things started to change.

II
AFFIRMATIONS

People who try affirmations are doing so because they have a perception of "lack." In other words, you are trying to convince yourself of something. The first thing you should do is understand yourself. In other words, if you have scarcity issues in your life, no amount of affirmations will help. The reason for this is your belief in scarcity. If you wish to convince yourself of abundance in that area, your view of "lack" will always undermine your affirmations.

Why not concentrate on the abundance in your life? Too often, we look at what we don't have, measuring that against what others have. Others who seemingly have everything may also be unhappy because they experience a different life deficit. Look, be grateful for what you have, and develop a want for the things you have. Practicing this would ultimately make you far more satisfied, and you will start to experience abundance in your life.

In the late 1970s, much was made about positive affirmations. I, too, indulged in them. I was pretty disappointed in spending money on some of these workshops without any "positive" results. No Jaguar for me! However, I realized two things as I went away from quick fixes. I could not change my beliefs by repeating and posting affirmations around the house; I didn't need more. The only way that I could make positive changes is within myself. I noticed that I would have these positive affirmations while underlying it. I said, "No, you don't," or "That doesn't work for you."

I came to realize that what I needed to change was my belief. So instead of wanting a more prestigious car, a bigger house, and more money, I reassessed how I looked at my thoughts.

I concluded that I really didn't need a better car. My house was quite adequate to raise four children, each with their own space, and I had enough money to live far better than many people. In other words, I shifted my point of view. It went from what I wanted to what I needed.

So, I started being grateful for what I had instead of dissipating my time and energy on the outside world and comparing myself with those who had more. I concluded that not having the most toys was okay. It was about living within our means and enjoying the fruits of our labour to the max. It was my brain and ego that pushed me to seek more.

I have found that we want what we don't have and are ambivalent or indifferent about what we do have. The reason we do this is due to our focus on the lack rather than on abundance. Most advanced people don't suffer from deficiencies, regardless of how little we perceive them to have. Others have ample wealth yet are not tied to it. Still, others continue accumulating money (I distinguish between wealth and money) because earning money for its own sake is poverty consciousness. Again, spiritual or not, they are not fully aware if they have tackled the issue of lack in their life.

III
POINTS OF VIEW

In some circles, there are beliefs that life is pointless. We cannot control events and circumstances, so what is the point in even trying? This kind of thinking is all about me and not thinking of other people's needs. All that there is to it is self-destructive thoughts that can lead to diminished enjoyment in life. Instead, think of what you can contribute.

There are approximately 7.8 billion people on the planet with roughly 7.8 billion different experiences; collectively, they make up the world. As a result, the more people we get to know, the more we can share individual experiences, giving us a much broader picture of experiencing humanness. The world is not groundless, neither figuratively nor literally. Embrace the world; get out there; interact with as many humans that are different from you and start to experience all the world has to offer. You do not need money to do this. Go out in your backyard and enjoy the feeling of the blades of grass on your feet. If you live in a condominium or apartment, visit your nearest park.

Most people are obsessed with weeds on their lawns. I have grass that is full of dandelions, and I love the expanse of yellow over green, besides it is good for the bees. I love cloud formations; I love the challenges work brings to me. There are so many things that can be awe-inspiring. We just have to look and change our way of thinking.

A point of view can also be a source of judging others' beliefs or our own. For instance, we think of having illusions as a negative notion that we must get rid of. Heaven forbid we should be delusional. Well, to some degree, we all are. At least, we think others are, while we are bountiful of sanity. Aren't these thoughts we have determined to be negative, thus trying to eliminate them? First, how do you know they are illusions and delusions unless you have already decided they are? Therefore, there is no point in trying to get rid of them. That only keeps them around longer and makes them more concrete. Just let them go. You have thousands of thoughts in a day (probably more), yet most of those float by, many we are not even aware of. But occasionally, a thought comes up that we make meaningful. We spend more time with that thought than necessary, giving it energy. Some cogitations we decide are pleasant, and others we don't like, so we try to push them away.

In all instances, they are all thoughts, and we should be able to determine how much energy we should give them. We worry about something that has been decided to be an illusion or even a delusion. We offer illusions and delusions (which are not real) more energy and thought than needed. Let them go!

IV
ATTITUDE

Some people had to endure a challenging childhood. I was one, but then again, I was an extremely contrarian child. My brother, on the other hand, was 180 degrees different. Which means he did not suffer the same slings and arrows I did. However, I forgave myself for being the way I was and forgave my father for reacting to me in the manner that he did. Later, I also apologized for the way I was. This had a tremendous healing effect on me. I also understood that my father loved me unconditionally. He was simply exacerbated with me and did not know how to handle it. Frankly, neither did I, as a parent. I can only be thankful that none of my children were as bad as I was growing up. Parents learn on the fly. As many books as there are written on this topic, they do not cover all the variations a child brings to the table or the emotions each of them may elicit.

It is time you forgive yourself. You are not the person you were as a child; no one is. Let go of thinking you are not worthy because you are. Focus on your accomplishments and use them to validate yourself. You are the only one that can be you; you have a special place on this Earth. Regardless of what anyone thinks, we all have "faults." That should never be the limiting factor. Love yourself for who you are. Love the fact that you have the experience (and privilege) of being human. Too often, we carry around hatred towards our parents because they were abusive. They may very well have been, and we should also understand that sometimes they were trying to do their best under trying circumstances in their own lives. Concluding that the issues they were dealing with are not yours, move forward. Forgive yourself and your parents and move on.

Choose your attitude. If your parents are deceased, you can still forgive them. Your energy will enter the universe.

The opposite of positive is negative. The two balance each other out. The reality is that both are judgements unless you are talking about physics. Does feeling "good" matter every single day? Do you decide on your attitude each day? When you wake up and look at the weather, do you decide, "This is going to be a downer day?" The question is, why would I do that? Why can't you summon up from that same place, "This is going to be a terrific day?" It becomes a mindset.

Choose to be happy each day and bring happiness to all you do. I discovered many years ago that if I relied on other people or events to make me happy, each day would be akin to throwing a dart at a moving target and expecting happiness as the outcome. Not choosing your attitude, your mood will be based on results not in your control. Better to simply bring your joy to people and events. That way, you are assured of being happy more often than not.

V
ASSUMPTIONS

We make assumptions about many things; many of them have to do with our laziness, so we simply accept what is. Before Christopher Columbus, the widely believed and accepted "assumption" was that the Earth was flat. He challenged that notion.

In 1543, Nicolaus Copernicus discovered that the planet was not the centre of the universe, as was the assumption of the day. In fact, the Earth rotated around the sun. Despite that, it took another century for this to take hold. In 1633, the Catholic Church forced Galileo to recant the theory that the Earth revolved around the sun. It wasn't until 1979 that the church finally admitted it was wrong.

We "assume" that religious books tell us the truth. Challenging those "assumptions" would be asking many questions. For instance, who is the author? Who made this person an expert? What authority tells you not to believe anything other than what is written in these books? What is the premise for telling you not to look beyond something written thousands or hundreds of years ago or yesterday? We live in a fluid and ever-changing universe. Why do we stick with beliefs that have been disproven through science? When our parents tell us something, do we challenge those assumptions? Where did they get their information? Did they get it from their parents or others? Is it just hearsay? We assume that just because someone claims an absolute truth on the internet, it actually is. However, this may not always be the case. The other day, I was reading about a politician looking to lead her party. She challenged people that disagreed with her point of view even though they were not conspiracy theorists, and as proof, pointed to a book written by someone to prove her point. I was shocked because this was a supposed intelligent lawyer. Just because someone writes something in a book does not mean you can assume it is any more accurate than someone's words. We need to fact-check the credibility of our sources.

That is why it is important to question assumptions.

Finally, we know that parts of the bible were written by Jesus's disciples. Therefore, we assume that what they wrote, is God's truth. The problem is that just because we hang around with someone, doesn't mean that we know what is going on inside them. There are experiences we have that can only be pointed to. I use that bicycle analogy, where explaining to someone how to ride, will not translate into riding. It is only conceptual. The Ten Commandments are a doorway into living a better life, but following them will only get you so far. Your experiential journey will be different. It is the main reason why I contend the bible cannot be taken literally. If one does, one is disconnected with humanity. Many spiritual leaders are highly judgemental. Strange, since the bible tells us not to be. There will always be dichotomies in the bible, because so is life. We have to decide what works for us, not for everyone else.

VI
CONFUSIONS

Sometimes we confuse what we feel with others' emotions. For instance, someone is angry with you; they are the angry ones, yet suddenly we feel anger towards them. This is called sensory processing sensitivity. I speculate that thoughts are like radio frequencies. That is, we not only have our thoughts, but when the correct frequency hits us, we tend to hear other thoughts from who knows where. This is not about listening to other people's frequencies to get what they think about you. When you dial into a radio frequency, you get the music on that station; however, you don't necessarily get the specific song you want to hear at that moment.

As it is with thoughts, I don't know how they manifest within us. For me, they are not necessarily voices but floating in as thoughts. For others, they may be voices. That is why we should sit back and evaluate them and not give them meaning unless we can use them.

Thus, it is with thoughts; how to let them flow. The best way is to let them be. Don't judge them; just notice them and continue with your actions. If you leave your realizations alone, they will leave you alone. You have several of them each day, yet you may not remember or even be aware of most of them. Let your thoughts go. What makes them linger is the meaning you give them. Some we make more significant than others. Suddenly, you say, this one is important. But it is you that decides that. It may be relevant because you deem it a dirty thought, one you shouldn't have, or you just thought about starting a business. Now you want to let that "bad" thought disappear. However, you gave it energy by making it meaningful. Therefore, it will hang around until you let go of the judging, which will neutralize the thought. Otherwise, that thought expands, and you think, "I can't start a business because I have all these terrible thoughts; thus, I am a dreadful person."

Our institutions have people who claim to have heard voices asking them to harm others. They very well may have, but we still need to distill them through acceptable societal behaviour.

We tend to judge thoughts as good or bad; they are simply thoughts. They tend to hang around by giving them meaning, thus changing our mood. Besides, we still have within us the capacity to ignore those thoughts or voices. Letting them go instead of trying to block them will go a long way towards dissipating those urges.

Our thoughts flow through our brains all day long. Some we may not be aware of, others we are slightly cognizant of, hence giving them meaning and ultimately judging; why else give them meaning? "Oh, that one is important." "Where did that thought come from?" Wow, that thought was horrible." "Mm, this thought arouses me." "Wow, what a great idea." "Oh, that is so gross." "I must be a bad person to have thoughts like this."

All those thoughts are nonsense. The fact is, we don't control our thoughts any more than our ability to regulate the wind. What determines the strength of our cognition is what we do with them once there. Don't judge it; say thanks for the idea and move on. Regardless of the "bad" conclusions we come to. Know that you are not your thoughts. Underneath it all, you know who you are. Have those so-called evil thoughts. They do not define you unless you let them and give them meaning. The difference between those in institutions and those that are not, is their actions with those thoughts.

VII
DIALOGUE OF THE MIND

I have internal discussions all the time. It seems as natural as breathing. What is important is what we do with the information. For instance, I may judge a situation or a person, and what my mind is talking about is judgment. I then shift my thinking to how does this judgment relate to me. After all, we tend to judge others by our own shortcomings. It usually doesn't take long for another internal discussion.

Internal dialogue happens when evaluating a strategy or a situation; there simply is no end to thinking and internal conflab.

It is difficult to say how to let your mind be or just float along without stopping and entertaining it. It's impossible to provide a definitive answer to that; it is like asking how you walk. You can say put one foot in front of the other; however, something has to give rise to moving your feet. Saying the brain commands it, is only pointing to it. How does the brain decide to move the feet? What triggers the brain as you want to cross the street? What neurons in the brain fire up my legs? Do I have to give my brain a request to move my legs? Clearly not! Scientists and doctors may know the answers to these questions; we just walk.

What part of the brain is activated to look and interpret what we are looking at? I grew up in an era where analog television was king. We got our first television in 1958. Before digital televisions and cable, there was a lot of "snow." We had to see the images through the snow patterns. Once my eyes became accustomed to watching television, I never paid attention to the background snow anymore. Before that, someone had to point out the images. It could not be done by asking, "How" do I see the pictures? So, seeing is also a learned phenomenon. (We cannot see what we do not believe). Asking how you see becomes problematic.

If you asked me how to meditate, I could say sit with your legs crossed or not and do nothing for the next half hour. It is really that simple. However, when you do meditate, you experience a lot of things. But they were not in the instructions: "How do I meditate?" Understanding becomes apparent as you continue meditating. For instance, as a child, I was told we have thousands of thoughts. I remember thinking, "That's ridiculous; I don't have thoughts." I never noticed that I had that thought or any other. The mere fact that I thought I didn't have them; well, you see where this is going. Things become apparent when we become ready to see them.

VIII
THINKING

"Negative" or unwanted thoughts come and go. We really have no control over what comes into our heads. Resisting these thoughts gives them energy. Acknowledge them, and then let them go. Focus on something else to keep you in the present moment. Start paying more attention to those things that are agreeable to you. Look for beauty in everything. Be grateful for what you have and never mind what you don't have.

We usually limit our capacity to understand and create relationships when we judge people. Humans are multifaceted and sometimes behave in ways others disapprove of. That doesn't mean anything. At that moment, you displayed an idea or attitude that was disagreeable to someone. That doesn't define us. Nor does another person's perspective or attitude towards us characterize them. If we let go of judgment, there is no negative or positive, good or bad, like or dislike; there just is. You can be joyful and happy, all from within. It starts with non-judgment.

Why hang onto "negative" moments or events? The longer we hang onto them, the longer it takes for us to enjoy the present moment. Significant or not, memories are no longer bona fide; they only exist in the mind, and the mind can play tricks with memory as well. If you have siblings, you may remember a significant event differently even though both of you were present at the same event at the same time. It doesn't mean either of you was wrong; it just means that your brain processed the information differently. That is also why two people going down the rapids in Colorado have differing experiences. One will find the journey exhilarating, and the other one will hate it and wonder why they ever agreed to go rafting in the first place. Again, it is merely how we process experiences, in other words, our programming.

It is essential to understand that the mind cannot always be trusted. Therefore, why add your own evaluation to your experiences? Even the word significant can be judgemental, and it may be substantial at the time, as it is monumental for a five-year-old to be waiting for a "significant" holiday to roll around.

We judge ourselves when we have "negative" thoughts. The reality is, we do think. Because we have decided something is negative, we have to eliminate it. Thinking comes and goes; we determine what we hold onto because it means something. We also provide the meaning. Letting thoughts be and letting them flow (as most thoughts do) will leave us alone.

There is a saying that goes, 'That which you resist persists.' This saying is rooted in physics. For every action, there is an equal and opposite reaction. Hence, the more you push against something, the more that something will exert itself back with an equal force. If you are unfamiliar with this, try applying pressure against a concrete wall with both hands. You cannot move the wall because the wall is pushing back with an equal force to yours. Of course, the wall only pushes back up to the pressure put on it. Similarly, if someone applies pressure against you and you resist, you can only hold off your opponent if you have the energy to do so.

Along the same lines, if you try getting rid of your thoughts, they will continue to be there with an equal determination to remain. The wall ceases to push back when you stop; your thoughts cease to stay if you let them flow through you.

And then there is overthinking. In my experience, the mind chatters less when talking to people or doing something. Overthinking is something that can be overcome with practice. Noticing a lot of brain activity? Start focusing on the present moment. What am I doing? Go into the minutest details. If walking, what do the surroundings look like, feel like? How does the bottom of the foot feel? Are you walking heel to toe? If so, how are you transitioning between the heel and toe? How do you transfer your food to your mouth when eating? Do you use a fork, spoon, or chopsticks? How is the food being transferred onto your utensil? Did you notice the colour of your food? Notice the texture of the food. How does it smell? What does it taste like once it hits your tongue?

All these things will keep us from overthinking. When focusing on what is in front of us, our minds will slow down automatically. That's because we are engaged in this moment. When trying something for the first time, or the first several times, our mind has less chatter going on. Our brains work in overdrive before starting, wondering if we can get this thing right. What happens if I don't, and so on? Once we start a project, our mind tends to keep quiet unless we pause. Then it starts adding more doubt for you to contemplate.

IX

EGO

Is ego real? Is the Devil Real? Where does the ego get its start? It is awakened when we tell people how good they are without merit. We compare people; we judge people; we are better than others; we are entitled. Sound familiar? Probably, but that is not us. We are not that good; we are not worthy; we have evil thoughts, so we must be dreadful or, at best, imperfect. People do not equate this with ego, but it is also ego-driven. What about the reverse? When you start thinking of how honest you are, how humble you are, or all the remarkable philanthropy you do, isn't that also ego-driven? You are trying to convince yourself when you must tell people how wonderful you are. For instance, when you tell me that you can't stand liars, it tells me that you lie. That leads to the notion that you don't like yourself. After all, if you don't like liars, and you lie, you can't like yourself either.

For most people, thoughts are legitimate; thus, so is the ego. We never get rid of the ego, and to suggest otherwise is the ego talking. The best advice I can provide is to be mindful of your ego and differentiate it from your true self. Ask yourself, "Does the information I am imparting make me look better in the eyes of the receiver?" If so, then you might know it is ego-speaking. Being shy is a form of egoistic being, basically saying that you are not as good or worthy as those you are being shy with. Beating yourself up because you made a mistake is also ego-talking. When you say, "I am not worthy," or "People don't like me because…" (fill in the blank), chances are that's your ego speaking. Once you learn to recognize your ego, you are a little more at choice, whether you want to listen to your ego or not. No matter how good you get at recognizing when your ego is at work, it comes up from time to time, regardless of how evolved you are or think you are. In some Quora discussions, people asked about attaining enlightenment. The ego's desire for wisdom and understanding is to differentiate from "common," "unenlightened" people. Professors usually depart knowledge; a professor seldom comes along to impart true wisdom.

You can't eliminate the ego, but you can control it.

What some people think of enlightenment is simply an "aha moment." Every time we delude ourselves into thinking the ego is gone, we understand that the mere thinking we have rid ourselves of the ego is the ego talking. When we get past that, we can accept who we are, with or without ego. The ego rarely goes away for any length of time, if at all.

The first obstacle is realizing the "I" is not who we really are. The better description would be "we." We are brought up to think in individual terms. Everything we do or say refers to "I did this" or "you did that." You see, we are also limited by language. We always refer to an individual as "you" or other pronouns. A reasonable analogy is the Star Trek series, where they introduce the Borg. The Borg is a collective hooked up by a computer to have a single thought. We are that from a spiritual perspective. However, the human experience sees us as individuals, and that fierce belief ties us to our ego.

Once we see ourselves as a part of a higher experience, we can, perhaps, tame the ego. The ego never really goes away, but there is a greater chance of letting it be when we become aware of it.

When Christ talked about being tempted by the "devil," (The King James version, Mathew 4:1-11), He may have been speaking of the ego.

I wish to clarify that the ego is not separate from the mind; in essence, it is the mind in the same fashion as the river is the water you drink. However, the mind does not always align us with spiritual needs.

X
JUDGEMENT

When I arrived in the mid-fifties in this country, I experienced a great deal of prejudice from my friends' parents. I did nothing but go to school with their children. I was not prejudicial towards any racial groups or had anything to do with the war. I started to understand why they were this way when I got older. Many had lost siblings and friends to the war and were still hurting. They suffered from Post Traumatic Stress Disorder decades before they knew it was a thing. I happened to be a lightning rod for much of that anger. We may sometimes become prejudicial when we talk about a group of people we know nothing about. That is, we tend to pre-judge them. None of us can possibly know all the Jews and Muslims globally or what type of people they are. There will always be good and evil in every society. If we happen to know a few based on newspaper readings or friends' experiences, we assume that the entire race or religion is that way. When I first came to this country, there were very few blacks (only one family in Hamilton) and no South Asians. Our community had a few Chinese and Japanese, but that was it. The rest consisted of European immigrants.

We sometimes forget that Canada, by its very design, is multicultural. Unlike countries, through the invasion of Europeans, we instantly became multicultural and continue to this day because of our immigrants. Our way of life is based on the quilted fabrics that make up this great country. Suggesting that certain groups are not welcome because they are different is anti-Canadian.

The "founders" of this nation took over this land through genocide—the indigenous inhabitants were pushed off their lands and marginalized to reservations. They were further diminished and traumatized when their children were taken from their parents and sent to residential schools away from their communities to convert them from growing up as "savages." Our forefathers have really nothing to be proud of. If anything, history should teach us to be tolerant of others and their beliefs. To this day, we compare them to how they should embrace **our** lifestyle, the one that destroyed the environment and lives at dis-ease with nature instead of harmony.

Making fun of people who wear headdressing makes us all lesser people in society; we are really those same people disguised as Christians, Buddhists, Muslims, etc. Our laws are in place to protect those who cannot protect themselves; the marginalized sections of society.

I have not seen laws in the North American culture which suggest Christmas should be removed. Why do we have prayers in publicly funded schools? Any public institution should remain secular; that is the inclusive way. Those that wish to educate their children in religion should do so through their own religious institutions.

There are laws, and they should be respected. However, hopefully, we will never have laws restricting people's fundamental rights to practice their religion (wasn't that one of the reasons immigrants came here in the first place?). Those who suggest that this country should adhere to extremist beliefs have failed thus far. "Honour Killings" have occurred in this country and are fully prosecuted. Sharia Law has not been passed because we have set our own rules of living and laws to follow. It certainly doesn't mean that we should stick to those laws no matter what. If something is out there that works better, why not? If the law works, then use it. But if it breaches one of our fundamental rights, we should be prepared for the consequences.

Canadians (who have been among the most generous globally) are starting to change their minds about minorities in our society because of their personal lack.

If we start by loving ourselves, we may have some to give others. Just because we don't always agree with people's points of view is no reason to judge them. In some beliefs (even those with extreme judgment issues), this is God's job.

We judge what is positive and negative; we determine likes and dislikes and what is meaningful in life; it is all in our control. Why not start with judgment? 'It is easy to stop; just stop,' that is easier said than done. But start noticing how we judge ourselves and our thoughts. Notice how much more energy thoughts are given (We do not control our thoughts, but we control the energy and meaning we give them). The more we fret about them, the more they will stay with us and mess with our minds. Don't judge; leave thoughts alone. Leaving them alone, thinking will leave us alone.

When we expand who we are and see to "others," we express our true selves. In the sixties, there was an expression, "Look after your family first." It was pointed out to me how we needed an expanded sense of family. It should include our neighbourhood, our province, our country, our continent, and our universe. I concluded that I am all of those. That is why patriotism does not sit well. It is more of an 'us versus them' mentality.

Just because the universe is in perfect balance, it should not prevent us from assisting others. There is also a vast difference between helping and assisting. Helping never lets a person take ownership of the issue. On the other hand, assisting allows the person needing assistance to be in control and take ownership. Thus, we become an aide or an assistant.

When we look at the universe in balance, we tend to look at the poor, starving, and the mistreated from a perspective that someone needs to do something about. If God or the government is not helping, let's organize a group to help these poor people. The universe must not be in balance.

The truth of the matter is that the universe is in balance. All those people who have been marginalized are an expression of who we are. There are many small ways that we can be of assistance. Honouring ourselves is honouring "others." Ask ourselves why it is essential to be respected. We may find it is because we have no self-respect, so we demand it from others. Compassion is the same. Once we understand that we have to be compassionate with ourselves, we see a difference between empathy and feeling sorry for someone. Feeling sorry for someone lacks compassion and understanding. When we honour ourselves, our views can begin to shift. The world is you. We are always the common denominator when viewing the world. We start by changing our outlook.

In my experience, "enlightened" people don't chase illusions. They deal with what is in front of them at the very moment in time. They see the bigger picture. Allow the universe to unfold as it should. We will wind up where we are going, regardless. It just might not look like it. For instance, our views of success include dreaming of a big house and lots of money. That is successful because that is the North American narrative. However, having a wonderful family filled with joy is what we really want. Yet, we continue chasing other successes without realizing we are already successful. We simply change the view. You see, we are always chasing what we do not have rather than pursuing what we have.

We all want to change the world into a better place with kindness, compassion, and love. Unfortunately, we all have different ideas of how that looks and how we get there. We all expect the other person or persons to change; it has nothing to do with us. One of our biggest challenges is shifting our belief system from those with different views. We need to provide compelling reasons to change their attitudes and beliefs. We cannot do this by forcing them to our point of view. Somewhere, we must find a way to appeal to their sense of logic and reasoning and work with that. Before saying they don't possess reason, let's rethink this. From their perspective, they are logical; we are not. We all justify what we do. Our jails and institutions are filled with people that have justified their actions.

There is also a line between balancing the universe and eradicating unwanted behaviour. For instance, evil cannot exist without good and vice versa. A perpetrator does not exist without a victim; peace does not live without war. Lack cannot exist without abundance.

All these things exist as part of the human experience. When we say we are against war, we give war energy. When we say we are for peace, we provide peace energy. When we say we are against violence toward women, we energize violence toward women. When we say equality and respect for women, we give power to those aspects.

Sometimes, we need to be careful about how we communicate. We can communicate in a way that gets people's backs up, which will never move a conversation forward. Find a way to connect with people, regardless of how offensive and repugnant they may be. You never know.

We tend to see ourselves as lacking, especially in the early years of development. People in their twenties think they already know so much, as it is with people in their teens. Pre-teens are also evolving and think they know more than their parents because of information gleaned from the media, society, social media, and friends.

We evolve at our own pace, making us, being human, so unique. That is why we should not judge. Think of someone that is studying life at a grade 6 level. They look at you in your second year of university studying quantum physics. Would you say they are flawed because you cannot have an intelligent conversation with the grade 6 students? Of course not. And, neither should the eleven-year-old student compare themselves to the university student and think they are inadequate. In your twenties, it can be said that you are a grade 6 student of life. You are comparing yourself with people with grades and life experiences much greater than yourself. Its the same in your adult life. You may have different experiences from someone whom you dislike because of their viewpoint. Just relax.

You are not flawed. You can make up whatever priorities you want. Your preferences will most likely change as you gain more knowledge and experience. That doesn't mean you were flawed, to begin with. You made those choices with all the knowledge and experience you have in your twenties. To go back to the grade 6 analogy, you wouldn't expect a perfect paper on the theories of relativity from that student. They will write what they think based on their knowledge and experiences at that age.

XI
LIMITING THE MIND

Not really, because we are limitless. We chose to be limiting. As Christ once said, you can do anything I can do and more. (Not a direct quote; see the Christian Bible section at John 14:12.). Many interpretations lean towards "He didn't mean that literally because he can create and we can't." There is a school of thought saying we can actualize and, in fact, have. As we look around, many people tell us that we cannot do what is doable. It starts with our parents and goes on from there. If you have high aspirations, your family may tell you they are not attainable. Then there is the school teacher that says you will never amount to anything. Your friends, too, will want you to stay at their level of achievement. It is only those who break out of this mould who succeed.

I was a low achiever in school and left when I was 18 in Grade 10. A few years later, I realized that I was more than that. So, I went back to school at age 24 and finished high school and college. After deciding to return to school, my father asked me if I was sure. After all, he said, you were never any good in school and now are leaving a well-paid job.

In the end, it is what you put your mind to, followed by action, that you discover that limits are self-made.

9

BEING PRESENT

Stop acting as if life is a rehearsal. Live this day as if it is your last. The past is over and gone. The future is not guaranteed.

Wayne Dyer

I

IN THE MIND

All things other than this moment are pure illusions. The mind cannot possibly settle down while it has thoughts about things that do not exist. Worrying about studies, money, and the future only exists in fanciful thinking. It is not part of the present; only the worry is based on eventualities or past events. They are all in your mind. A broken relationship is merely the universe telling you that the relationship no longer serves us. The association is in thought only. Consider the following scenario. Think about the number of times you have worried about a loved one or how many times you have been concerned about money. I have yet to hear about worries solving issues. If you can do something about it, then do something! Worrying is just an excuse to feel bad. Then you can tell everyone, "Look how bad I am feeling," or, "Can't you see how stressed out I am?" As though somehow it excuses you from doing anything. Your mind may wish to suggest that you are not in the past or future, as you are thinking these things now. You are stressed now, not in the past, so you are living in the present. That is delusional thinking of the brain. The mind does not reside in the present; doingness does. You may say that planning is a task in the present. This is true, but planning neither gives you stress nor worry. It is when you stop and start worrying about if your plan is good enough that you enter into the realm of drifting into the future- Think. A good plan should not require you to worry if it is good. You should know that.

Can you imagine what it would be like if the future was real? We are in the business of making the future real. By worrying about it or being so excited about its coming, you can't wait; you miss out on this moment. Think about it, if we are such predictors of future outcomes, why not spend time in the casinos or the racetrack? Buy plenty of stocks. There is no future because we are in the present. Once we experience this, we can slowly start letting go of subsequent times. Living in the present moment allows us to experience much more peace and far less stress.

Stress or anxiety often comes from thinking about everything other than what is happening in the 'now.' Failing to be present will cause a range of emotions, many not good.

II
THINKING

Overthinking is habitual. The problem is that while you are busy thinking about what was and what may be, you are not engaging in creativity. Worrying actually stifles doing something. As an example, years ago, I was given a problem to resolve. I was assured that when the time came, they would all be there to support me in whatever I needed. As the time drew nearer, I realized that I was totally on my own. The reason was, that all the "helpers" were more interested in saving their careers, rather that being associated with a problem that seemed a sure loser. Once the problem was fixed, they all came out to congratulate me on an outstanding job. The point here is, that fear of failure prevented them from taking action. That is having your mind in the future, which holds nothing but illusions.

Worrying about our next mortgage payment and losing the house, we worry about something, not in the present moment. Imagine being in a bank and wondering how you will make ends meet. Suddenly, you are confronted by a bank robber. Now, we are no longer worried about events of the future, i.e., the mortgage loan repayment, etc. If we are not doing anything in this instance other than thinking, shift the awareness to breathing. That will bring us back to the present moment. It is why we suggest focusing on breathing when meditating. It keeps us in the moments of now.

Recently, I was talking to a friend of mine, and he said that he can't see people who just hold their cups in a particular way or have their tea just so. He said that he loves his morning coffee and just drinks it as soon as it is ready. We discussed the purpose of ritual and pouring a cup of coffee or tea. For instance, I warm my mug before I add coffee. To me, it isn't about doing things the right way (or wrong way). It is about being mindful of what you do. If you are aware of the little things, you will also become conscious of the big things you do. It is about disciplining the mind.

When I mentioned "discipline," I could see an expression of disapproval. That was okay, too. It is one thing to make people aware, but I disapprove of telling them they must or should do something (unless they are working with me and we need a desired outcome).

The same applies to the entire book: if you are reading it, I would prefer you ponder it rather than take it as something you should do.

III
BEING CHILDLIKE

To be clear, that does not mean being impulsive. Young people tend to do that. While living in the present, they also want things at this moment. This is what separates some adults, not worrying about what isn't or what could have been. We anticipate Christmas as soon as Thanksgiving is finished. Yet Christmas is over in an instant. We find that the weeks leading up to Christmas are exciting. It is not so much about the day but the preparation. And that happens in the present.

The problem arises when there is an anticipation of how things will turn out. The excitement of the parents as the child opens the gift. The excitement on the child's face as they tear open the wrapping or pull the colourful tissue out of the gift bag. The parents anticipate seeing their child filled with joy while the child is eager to find out what he got as a present. However, when the time arises, things can get disappointing when it does not fulfill the anticipation we were harbouring. We tend to make Christmas about presents rather than family and the love and joy of having everyone there. (In the U.S., the family and friends get-together happens more at Thanksgiving, which is a bit more focused, as there are no presents). Children look at the wonder of things. The period leading up to Christmas was exciting. They wish to bring that excitement to their children when they grow up. Some children may not have had a good experience during Christmas. They will carry that memory into their adulthood. The opportunity for adults is to create joy and excitement for themselves and their families. Just hang around childlike people.

I purposely left Christ and religion out of Christmas because I have noticed that families with different religious backgrounds also tend to get into the "Christmas Spirit."

10

SPIRITUALITY

The spiritual journey is individual, highly personal. It can't be organized or regulated. It isn't true that everyone should follow one path. Listen to your own truth.

Ram Dass

Spirituality is a brave search for the truth about existence, fearlessly peering into the mysterious nature of life.

Elizabeth Lesser

I

OBSERVATION

Both quotes resonate with me and complement each other; thus, I considered them appropriate to include.

You will know your "observer" more intimately along your spiritual journey. The mistake many people make is they think that a spiritual awakening is something other than achieving greater awareness. They believe spirituality is achieved in an instant. However, it is quite the opposite. It is a nuanced, slow process with high virtues in the longer run. When that awareness comes to you, you may think it was instantaneous. When I think of the overnight success of musicians, it really isn't; it came about through many years of practice and sacrifice.

Removing a spoonful of water from a pond does not make a noticeable difference. However, if you keep drawing water, eventually, you will see the pond has receded. So it is with your spiritual journey. You may not notice much difference as you walk along the path, but one day you will awaken because you can finally see differences in how you perceive things and react to situations. Once that happens, you will most likely conclude that **you** are the observer, and it will never leave you.

Although enlightenment is a gradual process, there are moments of clarity. For instance, I became aware of the planet and how it is perfectly balanced. I cannot describe my feelings much beyond pointing them out. There was a calmness and a sense of knowing. I had always known intellectually that the universe was perfectly balanced, but this was the first time I experienced it deeply to my core. That is not awakening, but rather an "aha" moment. If we are not careful, we may walk around telling others that we should let fate run its course because the universe is unfolding as it should. While this may be true, we must be cautious as it was our own experience. Others may have their own experiences, but we view the world from our own perspective. Since everything is in balance, we do not need to fix anything; we can only fix what is within us. The fact is that everything matters. If we start using our experiences as justification for our questionable behaviour, we have nothing but a thought that can be used as a weapon of inaction. Through meditation, we can find inner peace, which comes from within and starts with us. We need to focus on fixing ourselves rather than the environment. By doing so, we become far more mindful of polluting the atmosphere, wasting water and food, being aggrieved and becoming the aggressor and simply lessening our footprint.

We tend to view things as good and evil, but one cannot exist without the other. For example, the sound of music cannot exist without silence, as there is silence between the notes. Try listening to the spaces between notes; it is a fascinating experience. Victims cannot exist without a perpetrator, and good cannot prevail without evil. Starvation is not possible without satiation. However, just because these things are in balance does not mean they are okay. We only need to remove one in order to be in harmony. You see, one cannot exist without the other.

Thinking that one has spiritually awakened and looking for guidance in our behaviour following that "awakening" clearly means the awakening hasn't arrived. We are on this planet to experience being human. When people begin to connect with who they are, they want to get rid of everything from before. Why? They are still the same person. We don't leave or renounce work because we suddenly discover who we are. We are not our ten-year-olds anymore, yet we do not exist without them.

When "awakening," an outcome is being more compassionate. It is not about our feelings anymore but about other people's feelings and needs. No one is superior to anyone else. We offer the world our true selves. We no longer need to assert our opinions unless asked; even then, the arguments become less presumptive and more about our experiences. We no longer need to hide from who we are or lie about events to avoid consequences. There is not another you in this world, so don't deprive the world of the gift that is you by trying to be someone else. Everyone has a purpose in this world, find yours, for you are the best you; being anyone else will only make you second best.

If awakening is such a big deal, why doesn't everyone seek it? Well, who says they are not? Just because it may not fit our picture doesn't mean they are not. Perhaps their basic needs haven't been met. Even some highly "successful" people tend to have many issues with fear, self-esteem, or anxiety. They may be driven by fear to get to the top. They are outward-looking when they could be looking inward. I knew a highly successful woman who became a Vice President of a large corporation dominated by males in the "C-suite." There was no question she could hold her own. Unfortunately, her drive came from wanting to please her father. She always felt that regardless of what she achieved, it was never good enough for her father. She eventually succumbed to alcoholism and couldn't maintain relationships. Basically, she lost focus on her natural abilities.

Giving up everything and going on a spiritual path would mean that life is not fulfilled; thus, looking for something else. There are a few tenets to having a fulfilling life. Be honest (opinions and judgments are not honesty). If a mistake is made with someone or something, clean it up. If something should be said to someone before it is too late, then do so. Reconcile with parents and siblings. Be complete each and every day. Don't carry "I wish I had ..." and get rid of judgment. This is the "spiritual path" to tread. We can't be looking outside of ourselves for what is already within us.

II
GOD

People cannot truly know who God is, as each person's concept varies greatly. Some view God as a deity sitting on a cloud, directing their lives and demanding goodness. However, this perception is inaccurate. People's understanding of God is shaped by their parents or religious institutions, relying on scriptures or other writings from the past. Unfortunately, people often overlook the fact that those who wrote about God in the past had a limited view of the world and did not comprehend concepts such as energy, the laws of the universe, and other evolving changes. When others challenge their beliefs, people often get upset and fail to question more. Many belief systems assert that God wants people to find themselves before finding him, but this idea has two problems. Firstly, once someone believes in something, there is no room for further discussion. Secondly, different religions proclaim that there is only one God, but in reality, there are 8 billion versions of God, as each person has their own image and experience of God. Therefore, when someone says they can help you find God, they are essentially helping you find their version of God.

People can't know who God is, especially when everyone has a different concept. Some think God is this Deity sitting atop a cloud (heaven) directing our lives and demanding us to be good people. It does not work that way. Most people understand God as parents or religious institutions have told them. They rely on scriptures or other writings from people of their times. For some reason, we negate everything that comes after that. The fact that people with a limited view of the world write about a God without understanding energy, the laws of the universe, and other evolving changes skew reality. When people like me write something contrary to their belief system, they get angry that we challenge them. We must wonder why people get so emotional about a different point of view. We really should question more. According to various belief systems, God wants you to find yourself and then find him. There are two problems with this assertion. First, once you "believe" something, there is no further room for discussion. The other issue is God. Some religions proclaim there is only one God. That is not true; there are 8 billion Gods. We all have our own image and experience of God. So, when someone says they can help you find God, what they are really saying is they can find "their" version of God.

Since the Bible tells us that there is only one God, am I to assume that my version trumps all others? After all, it seems there are as many Gods as there are beliefs about what or who God really is. To put a finer point on things, suppose I tell you my car is red. You will immediately associate the colour with how you perceive red. After all, there are many shades of red, and you may even find a group of people that agree with your version of red. Because there are so many shades, you wouldn't know the actual colour unless you physically saw it. Even then, the colour is filtered through your vision. If you are colour-blind, it may be different yet again. The reality is, whatever the colour, it is a car with pigmentation. That is the truth. The rest is conjecture, not unlike having one God. There may be one God (or not), and how we perceive him is different.

Just because people feel good by going to a church, synagogue, temple, or mosque doesn't necessarily mean they are doing God's work. This is especially true when people leave these places and curse others for cutting them off in traffic. There are many different beliefs, even within the same religion, as not all adhere to the same philosophy. For instance, there are various Christian sects, Jewish sects, and Muslim sects, with each sect believing they are on the right path to God. Similarly, Buddhists also believe that their sect is "the one." Even atheists have their own beliefs about the existence of God. In reality, there are as many different views of God as there are people.

The point of all this is to say, relax; you are doing exactly what God wants you to do. It is not about being good or evil; it is about life's experiences. If your experience is to climb a mountain, so be it, and if it is to remain in prison for the rest of your life, you will gain knowledge in that aspect of humanity.

There exists only one soul, not higher or lower. That's sort of like saying there is a lower and higher God. How things affect people is incredibly personal. Sometimes, what we see in meditation are illusions. If there has been no physical effect, then let it go. It is the mind that brings meaning to everything we do. Giving significance to someone or something does not alter the event or object. We cannot take something that works for one person and assume it works for all. For instance, many people swear by crystals. It doesn't negate that. We should support people in finding peace and love, regardless of their path. The key is intention. If we look for spiritual growth or tranquillity within us, we have to intend it. The process is different for everyone. Intention is the process of moving an idea into action. The action seems to take us into whatever experiences and learnings we need to achieve our purpose.

The idea is to share your wisdom with those around us without expecting them to follow to the letter what we do, but some things will resonate, and they will use that to further themselves. So it should be for us. Taking things verbatim can lead to false beliefs. Regardless of how "spiritually evolved" someone may be, evaluate and see what resonates.

III

RELIGION VS. SCIENCE

The Bible is the singular truth for the three main religions. Christians, Muslims, and Jews believe you cannot accept anything but the written word. I respectfully disagree. There has been so much discovery over the years that religious leaders don't consider and turn a blind eye to. Nothing remains static. Unfortunately, leaders have been stuck in what happened thousands of years ago. Certain truths are written in these books. But we must remember that humans write all these books with their own biases. When modern-day philosophers or visionaries challenge some of these previous prophets, I must ask what the difference is. If someone speaks the truth, regardless of Christ, Mohammad or Dan Brown (Fictional, meant to represent modern times), the truth is still the truth.

For instance, we now know that the world did not start with Adam and Eve because it simply would not be possible, especially considering what taboo incest is (that's where science comes in). It is a metaphor; much of the Bible is written in metaphors. Yet, many people take these things literally. Whatever religious leaders we talk to, many have different interpretations. Besides, others merely regurgitate what their leaders tell them the truth is, regardless of the absolute truth. Most leaders preach the dogmatic aspects of their religion. They are often offended when hit with questions of the depth of our existence. Sometimes, it's to the extent of excusing themselves from the conversation.

When talking of matters of the heart, regardless of logic or science, we say that our heart matters more than our brain. Without our brains, we would not be able to negotiate a vehicle in traffic, and we would not be able to find our way home; the brain would not pump blood through the heart and so on. In other words, we cannot negate one over the other. It's the same with science and logic. We need all three (heart, science and reason) to get a complete picture. A singular view can never be right.

IV
ABOUT MASTERY

In the early 80s, I was at a weekend retreat with a leader I had met several times before. Because I knew him and what he brought each time we met, I decided to attend his weekend retreat. The purpose of the weekend was to discover who we are by simply asking the question, "Who are you?" We worked in pairs, and for ½ hour, each would ask the other that question. Then we switched and asked the same question to the other. After a couple of hours, we took a half-hour break and, during that time, continued asking ourselves the same question, "Who am I?" then, we would return to new partners and start the process over. You would think this question would evoke an immediate response, and it couldn't possibly last past an hour, but it took the entire weekend to get to the core of understanding who we are. The instruction was to present ourselves to the facilitator and tell him who we "think" we are. At that point, he would send us back to continue delving deeper into who we are.

Typically, we start by responding to the other person about our profession, perhaps degrees, family, and how we view ourselves. We tend to see ourselves through family, career and shortcomings, yet there is a much deeper self to explore. On the third day, miraculously, the room sounded like popcorn popping. One by one, everyone in the room got who they really were within twenty minutes of each other. And everyone had a different answer. Indeed, we are one and different.

My point here is two-fold. One, a leader can draw the best from us and spiritually connect us. The second is, you will note, that I referred to him as a facilitator or leader. That is very different from a master. I have sat in many meetings within the Tao movement. Infrequently, the "master," a female, in this case, referred to as "Lady Master," would be present. There was a male "Master" present from time to time. When I presented my views regarding spiritual matters during those times, I never referred to them as "master." All these people are on the same journey as all of us. I prefer to call them facilitators.

We never master spirituality because that means there is nothing else to achieve. We can master tying a knot or master the art of painting, but we cannot, by its very nature, master spirituality. Therefore, I never refer to spiritual leaders by their titles. In other words, Father Bob is just Bob, and I refer to them as such. Similarly, you will never hear me call a spiritual leader "My Master" because they are not masters over me. They are teachers, all on a journey together. I, too, have facilitated some courses. I sometimes learn more than the students. When talking to others that have taught students, they say the same. I also had many teachers in my life. Some were not, by reputation, very nice people, yet they provided me with great insight into myself. Judging a book by its cover may not always be the best option because, after all, it is a "judgment."

V
PAYING FOR KNOWLEDGE

The question of why we need to pay for knowledge arose at different times, especially when it has to do with self-improvement or spirituality. Even those that provide learning, wisdom, or insight for free demand a lot from their "disciples." Despite everything, they still need to raise money to live. If it is of value, then pay the amount. If it is not, don't. It is pretty simple.

Car manufacturers have different prices for cars. If you don't want to pay a great deal of money, buy a less expensive car. But suggesting that Mercedes charge the same price as Ford doesn't make sense. You can argue that they both get you to a destination, and that is true. The quality may vary; that is what you pay. Universities charge varying prices. We don't judge Harvard's admission prices; we simply don't go there if we can't afford it or aren't smart enough to attain a scholarship.

It is the same with other learning, whether from a sage or someone who wants to impart wisdom for a fee. Why judge that?

The people who charge have spent time and energy coming to those conclusions. They have spent years learning and have gained a great deal of knowledge and skill over those years. They may get a job that pays. Not only that, but they will most likely go to the one that pays the most, all things being equal. It is ironic in a way, but you are willing to pay an exorbitant price to see a sports game and don't complain about the price or the fact that many athletes make more than CEOs of corporations. Yet, when providing insight into how your life works, you complain about the price.

Some professional athletes and entertainers get far more money in a single year than someone like Eckhart Tolle will make in a lifetime. His advice is far more relevant than most basketball players I know. It is incredible how we judge the value of people who impart knowledge and wisdom that make money, yet people who titillate our senses through sports and entertainment, are never mentioned in the same context; that is, they should impart their skills for free.

There is no point in judging people that make exorbitant amounts of money. Attending a sporting event contributes to their salary. Teachers are paid relatively poorly yet provide a lot more by contributing to society; they make a difference in our children and the future of our communities. Doctors and caregivers are there to administer to patients or save lives. Without scientists, we would still be living in the dark ages; there would be no sports medicine or analytics.

Perhaps we need to look at how we have programmed our priorities.

VI
A POINT OF VIEW

There are so many beautiful things on this earth.
Countless people are doing incredible charity work; millions
volunteer their time freely. Without volunteers, many of the
institutions we have wouldn't be functioning. Look around
and start seeing what is right in this world. Turn off the
news. Listen to your hearts more than skeptics. Our world is
a reflection of us. That which we give energy to expands.
We experience the dark night of the soul because that is
currently where our heart is at. We can always find negative
things going on. And when you pay heed to them, they
follow us around. I worked with a person that had trust
issues. It wasn't surprising that he gathered untrustworthy
people around him. His energy drew these people to him. If
we believe that the world is going to hell in a handbasket,
we will continue seeing those dark forces in our lives. Belief
is a powerful thing. Even the Bible mentions the power of
belief. When we believe something, we look around us for
support in those beliefs.

Start looking for beautiful things that are happening on
the planet. Surround ourselves with people that lift your
spirits instead of dragging them down. Change your outlook
and friends. See the world from a different perspective; we
will feel better and give more energy to those around us.

The world cannot exist without good and evil, dark and
light; eradicate one, and there becomes an imbalance.
There cannot be light without darkness; similarly, there
cannot be darkness without light. If there is only darkness,
how would you know if there is nothing to compare it to? We
need light to identify darkness. Once we see that, we can

choose to draw closer to either the dark or the light. If we select light, then we move away from the darkness.

Our body consists of multiple neutrons and electrons; when the physical body dies, the only energy left are quarks, which dissipate into the universe. While quarks retain memory, they are bits and pieces. So, if we reincarnate, then we may have different molecules making up our bodies and brains. We should really think of the mind as a computer waiting to be programmed to allow us to function as human beings. The input into that computer is based on the programming we receive as we grow up. And like any computer, it becomes obsolete after many years.

The story of God and heaven is exactly that, a story that has been passed from generation to generation. We tend to put history in terms of reality; history is really there to teach us how to conduct ourselves (or not) in the present moment. It has to be shown as legitimate; otherwise, we wouldn't take our actions too seriously.

Debates should never revolve around who is right or wrong. Take in the information, process it, and decide for yourself whether you accept it or not. It has nothing to do with being right or wrong because those are judgements. Otherwise, we are no different than a computer; we tell them what is right and wrong and how to interpret information.

Those who believe in the Bible and contemplate whether heaven or hell is better or worse for us won't change reality. Unfortunately, those that believe in a better place after death change their behaviour to accommodate those beliefs. For instance, I will go to heaven if I am good. I will endure this suffering because things will be far better when I die and go to heaven. God will look after me because I am a good person.

Similarly, I want to avoid going to hell. We don't always lead our best life by having all these thoughts, and we constantly worry if we are good enough to avoid hell. We cannot achieve perfection as humans. Of course, to avoid hell, you have to be a member of the right religion, as not all religions believe in heaven or hell. I have known many exceptional people who believe dying is where it all ends. That's it. Total oblivion. They live their life the same as all of us do. They support charities, are kind to their employees and neighbours, and are perfect candidates for "heaven." Except, they don't care. They have understood humanism and embraced it. They know what works and what doesn't in their lives, and they seem far happier than many people who believe that the afterlife will be with their personality and memory.

Physics tells us we cannot destroy energy. We are made of energy. When we die, our consciousness is in the universe; as a collective, we experience all that has passed before. If Karma is a form of judgement, a human trait, can it be part of our energy dissipating when we die physically? If so, this is the karmic past we think will pay retribution for our past lives. If none of us recalls our past lives, how do we know the Karma wafting around isn't someone else's judgement floating along? Humans are taught that we need to behave like God or Jesus at a very early age, and then they place impossible standards on us. Catholics believe they are born sinners, yet Christ supposedly came to rescue us from sin. They give us the carrot (heaven) and stick (hell) routine to keep us on the straight and narrow. There is no judgment. God knows you intimately better than someone else does. That's because you are the God of your universe.

For example, an infant or a senior leans too far back in a chair and subsequently topples over. The laws of the universe do not care if you are young or old, good or bad, with or without Karma, because it just happens when the rules of gravity have been violated.

VII
SEEING OTHERS DIFFERENTLY

Why is it that we can see faults in others much quicker than in ourselves? It is similar to our inability to see our nose or cheekbones unless we look outside ourselves to see them in a mirror. People are the same. They act as mirrors to us, so it is easier to see ourselves in others. When we tend to criticize others for their behaviours, there is a good chance that we harbour similar thoughts within us.

Let's look at racism as an example. Some people hate people of colour or different religions; we call them racist. Then, some hate racists. You can see the common thread here, hate! We may differ on reasons, but the bottom line is we have hatred in our hearts. The fact that both sides are coming from the same place, hate, makes no difference. I grew up as a European immigrant in Canada in the fifties. When we came over, there were very few people of colour. There were four prominent religions, Judaism, Presbyterian, Anglican, and Catholic.

Coming from Germany, I was an easy target, as people's emotions were still raw from the Second World War. I understand that. What I don't understand, to this day, is why we paint everyone with the same brush. It's the regime, not the innocent people. What about all the innocent Germans, Italians, Spaniards, or Japanese that had nothing to do with the Nazi regime? Painting all people with the same brush is what opened my eyes to hate.

Interestingly enough, one of the few people that showed a lot of love and compassion toward me was a Jewish family. We found a commonality. They spoke Yiddish, which has many similarities to German, so we could understand each other.

I noticed that white people also made much fun of other immigrants. Targets included Italians, Scots, Jews, and Polish people. I recall sitting in a grade 4 class and listening to a couple of immigrants, one Dutch and the other Italian, barely speaking English. Yet, here they were calling each other DPs, a derogatory term used to identify displaced persons.

I knew that I would eventually lose my accent. I was also mindful that people of colour, regardless of whether they lost their accent or not, would never lose their skin tone, thus always being a target of people who saw differences and not similarities.

Canada was always considered to be an inclusionary, tolerant society. I knew differently. Even though we had very few people of colour back then, it didn't stop many of my classmates from making jokes about Americans of African descent.

Jewish people were made fun of for their frugalness, as were people from Scotland. And, within Canada, there was much fun made of people in Newfoundland. In Germany, people of the far north (bordering The Netherlands and Denmark) were considered uneducated, and people in the South were considered backward.

You get the picture. People from all walks of life find something to dislike about someone, be it how they look, the clothes they wear, the religion they follow, the length of their hair, the lack of respect, culture, geography, and on and on it goes. It is human nature to find accepting something new and different difficult. Patience with difference arises only with practice and habit.

How many times have we read about a heinous crime and thought they should hang that person, put them in jail, and throw away the keys without ever listening to the facts or mitigating circumstances?

For all these reasons, it is vital to see ourselves in others. We, too, harbour ill thoughts, except we don't act upon them. Many times, we don't see ourselves that way. That is why we need to see others in ourselves and be honest enough to evaluate our contribution to society. We all have justifications for what we do; the jails are full of people with explanations. Doing the right thing requires us to go beyond our motives.

11

WHO ARE WE?

Knowing yourself is not so much a question of discovering what is present in ourselves but the creation of whom we want to be

Paraphrasing Mihaly Csikszentmihalyi

I

ABOUT US

The ego is sort of like the devil; it is not real. It is our mind that houses all thoughts and actions. We are both the witness of the observer and the observer. All of it is us. What we do, think, and conclude are all parts of the mind. Our mind is like a computer. It reacts to what it is programmed for. To separate ourselves from the computer, we must realize we act as one, a stimulus-response machine. We must understand that we allow outside forces to do our programming from childbirth. I'm not sure if we would allow someone to program our personal computer, but we do so with the most essential computer, our mind. Realizing that others have programmed our laptop, we can slowly start reprogramming it to our needs. After all, the process is slow; it took a lifetime of unwanted programming to get us to this point. It will take almost as long to debug and reprogram.

A transcendent moment came to me a few times. As a relatively young child, I guess the first was that the teachings in the Old Testament simply did not add up. Especially the story of Adam and Eve; it got me wondering if any part of the Bible was authentic. I started to view religion differently. The stories passed on from generation to generation have become quite distorted over the years. I have read the Bible twice since then and found that most of the Bible is written in metaphors. However, the religious teachings seem to take a more literal interpretation of the "Good Book."

For instance, if I look at the banishment of Adam and Eve from the Garden of Evil, I conclude that actions have consequences. You do not need to listen to what your inner voice (snake) is telling you; you need to weigh what is being said and accept the consequences of your actions. Since there are so many interpretations of what the snake represents, be it the devil, or sexual desire, it is really the mind that dictates your desires and feelings. Deciding to act on those thoughts and feelings is what gets many people in trouble.

Eden also seems to be an unrealistic utopia. When we are born, I suppose you can say that we are in a state of utopia. As we grow and develop knowledge, our mind moves away from utopia and starts to move towards trying to function in the world we are born into. When we encounter difficulties in life, we tend to think about a utopian life. Because everyone has a different version of utopia, the collective would never be able to get there. Some people may remember the days before computers and how life changed when computers were introduced. It was almost going to be a utopia. People wouldn't have to work, and robotics would care for all our needs. Seventy years hence, people are more stressed than ever. Go figure.

Some years later, I was fortunate to have spent some time alone, reflecting on myself, how I interact with others, how self-centered I was, and how indifferent I was to the plight of others. I also realized that we are spiritual beings having a human experience. That realization, coupled with an understanding that I created the universe in my image, caused me to see the world entirely differently. I ultimately started seeing the Bible from an altogether different perspective.

Of course, that little knowledge caused me to become an extreme idiot. Because I knew everything, I, of course, had to correct everyone else's thinking. Even though I knew they created their own universe, I was still caught up in arguing my points of view. In fact, I knew almost nothing. It was almost as if I had cracked open the door of all possibilities but had not entered. I peeked inside and saw the narrow view of a partially opened door.

Several years later, I had another epiphany. Out of the blue, I realized that the world was completely balanced. I realized at an experiential level that it had to be in harmony. We make judgments about good and evil, yet we can't have one without the other. As discussed earlier, light cannot exist without darkness, good cannot exist without evil, and both have their own values in this world. This time, I did not share my insights with anyone other than my wife because I knew better not to change someone else's experience of their life's path. I am not imposing my opinions, merely sharing an experience.

Finally, I discovered being in the moment. I understood this intellectually as I had read Eckhard Tolle's book **The Power of Now**. Intellect is different from experience. A good analogy is the difference between reading about riding a bicycle and actually riding one. Just because we read about riding bikes doesn't mean we can ride. Similarly, by reading any book, including this one, we may know something intellectually but not experientially. Even if you had a similar experience, it does not necessarily mean that your experience is the same as the writers'.

When I trekked through parts of the Himalayas, there were some treacherous paths one had to keep a real focus on. I could not think of anything other than just placing one foot in front of the other. It was an incredibly freeing experience. Since then, I have tried to stay focused on every moment in time and nothing else. I don't always succeed, but I return to the present when I catch myself drifting.

Through the process of living, I think I have become far more compassionate towards others and moved my attention away from myself, less impressing and more expressing; I have become a better leader and mentor to others. Mostly I know this in two ways, the results of interacting with others and the feedback from others. I accept people as they are.

The other day, I was asked to think about the difference between the ideal and the actual self. It was an interesting question, as we often have a quintessential view of self, which is different from our authentic self.

I said that the ideal self is an illusion. There is only one self, and that self already exists. However, it is just that idea that is an illusion. Which inherently means that we must work toward it to make it real. It cannot be anything real until we put the work in. Therein lies our responsibility to change the illusion into reality without getting swept away by the illusion and simultaneously accepting our authentic selves. Aptly put by Sophia Bush, "**You** are allowed to be both a **masterpiece and a work in progress,** simultaneously." It is a misunderstanding of who we are and our contribution to the planet. We sometimes look at religion to provide us with the ideal self. Then there are outside influences, including friends, parents, and strangers we read about, that influence our thinking about who we should be.

"You are allowed to be both a masterpiece and a work in progress, simultaneously."

Invariably, people who tend to be swayed by such thinking are not in touch with who they are. They think they are less than the unrealistic standards they and others have set for them. We have come to this world to experience being human. If we all share the same experience, we would have a narrow understanding of humanity, and our growth would be significantly impeded. Someone once said we should relax, for we are doing precisely what God expects us to do. If we plant a tiny apple seed, it grows into a tree and eventually produces fruit, as God intended. Imagine that tree getting stressed out looking over and seeing a peach tree and wondering why its fruit looks better than theirs. No, the apple tree knows it is an apple tree. And just like humans, not all apples are the same. Some are deformed; others are filled with worms. We see green, yellow, red, and multi-coloured apples; some are just right for someone.

So, why is it that humans fret so much over who they are? Because from the time we can remember, we have had expectations put on us by our parents, religious leaders, teachers, coaches, and peers. Very few allow children to be who they are and develop their own sense of being. Few teachers encourage their students to ask what they want to learn and why it is essential to them. Even fewer ask their children who they are and explore with them that they are not the labels others put on them. They pursue even fewer questions, such as why they are here in this country in this city at this given time. What is our purpose?

So, there is no ideal self; it is an illusion. And like many illusions, it can drag us down and take us away from identifying our only and authentic selves.

II
INDIVIDUAL VS. THE COLLECTIVE

When we look at a waterfall before the cliff, we see the river and water as one. When it goes over a cliff, it turns into a waterfall; looking closely, the water becomes a series of individual drops until it lands in the waters below, where it once again becomes the river. So it is with humans. We come from one source, go over a cliff and become fragmented until we die and become a stream again.

Do we know what our ideal self is? We have pictures of whom we want to be, yet they have nothing to do with who we really are. We tend to judge ourselves and think we should be someone else. Once we know ourselves, there is no "ideal" self left. Does a flower wonder what its ideal self is when it is just a bud? No, of course not. Neither should we. Life is a process. We cannot imagine how we will turn out in 30 years. Today we may think of a single relationship as the most essential aspect of life. Many years from now, we will realize that it is not just about a special relationship, but many of them that enrich our lives far more than we can imagine.

Taking the flower analogy further, a single flower can never be a garden; it takes many flowers to become one. Gardens I have seen also have a variety of flowers, making a garden. Similarly, many people make a community, but it also needs to be a mosaic, like the garden, to become a beautiful community. Unfortunately, we are so busy trying to make everyone the same as us that we fail to see the beauty in diversity. Singularly they are flowers; collectively, they become a garden. Singularly we are human; collectively, we are a community. To break it down even further, we are one with all of the universe at a sub-atomic level.

We are always our ideal selves at this point in time. We continue to evolve. There may be things we have done in the past that we are not proud of. Then again, if we hadn't done those things, we would never know or have compassion and understanding for those who do those things. Some parents forget that they were children and how they behaved, so they wish to prevent their children from doing the same. Parents don't understand that it is part of the growing-up process. They learn that the behaviour is inappropriate or will not serve them in society. We learn by making mistakes and by watching others. Parents tend to want their children not to make mistakes or get hurt.

We look at people and think, boy, they have it all together. We only see them from a distance; we don't know what is in their head other than what they wish to share. We see them as the ideal person we want to be. We are surprised when that person says, gee, I want to be more like you because we just wish we could be like them. We wish we were more like someone else. But this is a fool's game. Let's face it; we can only ever be second best to someone else. We are the best **us**, and no one can be **you** better than that.

This is a beautiful quote from psychologist Dan Gilbert. **"Human beings are works in progress that mistakenly think they're finished. The person you are right now is as transient, as fleeting and as temporary as all the people you've ever been. The one constant in our lives is change."**

The struggle between inner change and who we think we should be can be stressful. Think about the work environment where we are busy trying to impress those above us and prove to our colleagues that we are much more intelligent than we really are. At a work party, we try to impress the "boss" that we should be promoted, but we don't know that they are probably doing the same to their senior management.

We are the director of our movie, the actor within the film, and the audience, i.e., the observer. The audience of one is the person observing everything within us; we are all one. We cannot function properly without all these viewpoints in play.

By separating our "true self" from the other self, we essentially say that the true self is the head on a two-sided coin, where there is a head and a tail. That cannot be when you are the coin. One side cannot exist without the other. To say that one side is the real side is as much a fallacy as saying we have a "true" side.

The Bible alludes to all being one when Christ says he is the father, son, and spirit. What is meant by that (my interpretation) is that he is the creator (father), the son (human being), and the spirit (our source or essence). Many people will disagree, but this is how I look at the universe. I am responsible for all that I create in my life. Thus, I am the creator; my world is created in my image. It is so for all of us. The proof of that lies in the fact that when one dies, so does their universe. Yours continues with the illusion that the world goes on once people die. That's because it is your world, your creation.

From physics, we know that we cannot destroy energy; just transform it. Life-force permeates all of us. The people that go before us, leave their essence behind, becoming the same quirks and quarks that provide the energy to put us together as humans. As we grow, we continue creating more energy, which comes from wherever it is now and was before.

If there is a single source from which all power emanates, think of it as an image from a hologram. A holographic photograph is an image on a plate, and a laser beam is shot through the glass to project that image. If we break the glass in half, we still see the entire picture. No matter how small the pieces of the plate are, we still get the complete image, though it m

ay not shine as brightly.

Similarly, the source from which all spirits emanate is still the same spirit, even when broken down. The power may be diminished, but the same soul or life force remains. Combined with the use of the same energy to create physical bodies, this unites us all. Our software (the brain) creates the illusion that we are separate from one another. Other humans perpetuate this myth because it supports their ego-driven selves. Imagine how different things would be if we all realized we are one and the same. How can you argue with yourself? How can you say, "This is my country," or "Our country?" There would be no "against," so war would be impossible.

III
HIGHER SELF

I hear people talking about a "higher self." There is no "higher" self. Higher than what? Why do humans always want to separate themselves? I have my body, my mind and my soul. They are not separate; they are one. We cannot function when we miss one of these. The soul has the same significance as the mind. Without your brain, none of your organs will function. Behold the miracle that is you, in all its glories and non-glory. High does not exist if there is no low. You cannot live in a higher self; you can only live in all of you (yourself).

IV
IDEAL SELF

The "ideal self" is something that the ego or mind also makes up. The ideal self will always be out of reach. The reality is that there is only one self, and that is you. Do we get angry, of course? Do we get sad, of course? Do we get frustrated, of course? All those things make us human. Those that call them negative feelings are in a delusional world.

What is important is what we do with those emotions. Some aggressively demonstrate anger by looting, rioting, or beating up their loved ones. It means we should never get angry because we don't do those things. It is what we do with that anger that makes the difference. For instance, you can take that energy to write, clean up the basement or wash the floors. When sad, acknowledge the sadness and move on. Don't wallow in it. If frustrated, take a step back, take a deep breath and try from a different angle.

An individual I know is an incredibly kind and wonderful human being. However, when he gets frustrated, he breaks things, including his cell phone, television or anything else that frustrates him. In other words, he has very little patience. The proper thing for him to do here is to figure out what is not working and let that become the focus. You cannot do that with frustration; you must wait until you calm down before attempting to try again.

In short, you will have emotions that have nothing to do with the "ideal self." They are human experiences we all have to varying degrees, and what separates us is how we react to these emotions.

Undoubtedly, the theatre of the mind has written many plays. However, there is a constant. Who is observing the mind? Who is the one that sees the acting in this play? Who is that person that notices you as you are, without judgment? For convenience and talking with others, we call that "Self." We may wish to call it several other things, like universal consciousness or the essence that gives rise to humanity.

When it comes to life experiences, we shift from an actor in a play called Life, directed by others, to becoming the author, the director and the actor in our lives. It's easier to take responsibility for one's life when that happens.

Stop seeking external validation. This happens when we don't know who we are. Really!

Why do we wish to be more like someone else? Does it make sense that a tomato plant would want to be a tree? And yet, as humans, we would like to be someone else. The question tends towards not accepting who we are, so we want to be like someone else. I even heard someone say they wish to return as a dog in their next life. This tells me that the person's present life is out of control.

Let's start looking inward. Ask why we want to be like someone else. What is wrong with who we are? Begin taking ownership of our lives and look at how we wish to manifest ourselves from within. It begins with why we are on this planet and our purpose in life to fulfill our destiny. Take the focus off our needs and start interacting more with people. What qualities do we see in them that we already exhibit? What qualities that we don't like are within us? Are these reasons perhaps why we may not like ourselves? After all, if we don't like those qualities in others, why would we like them within us? So we tend to stop looking at ourselves and become self-righteous by hating others for thoughts that run through us.

Life is all about accepting who we are. We decide the person we want to be. Looking at others is like window shopping; we have to go inside (ourselves) to get what we want.

If we know nothing of ourselves, we are at the mercy of our reactions to outside stimuli. Whatever input is received from our surroundings, what we read, and the information given to us by our parents, siblings and friends will determine who we are. We can never be truly happy or confident in our actions because we will never be good enough. We set standards for ourselves that are unattainable. All the information about us comes from within when we know who we are. It's information that is independent of outside forces. When we compare ourselves with others, we find ourselves lacking. To measure ourselves against others is to be a sunflower longing to be a maple tree because it has more prominence.

Given that, how can the sunflower ever be at peace? It doesn't need the understanding to determine it is a sunflower. It understands its significance in life.

If we don't know who we are, does it not suggest that whatever we do, at best, can only be second to the real us? The inner us has a role to play, to offer our authentic self to the universe. To negate one's true self leads to a state of incongruence that ends in listlessness.

And finally, parents have told their children they are "special." This is to raise their self-esteem, but it is not the proper way to address issues of self-doubt. However, saying someone is special or unique gives the person a false sense of esteem. We are all special and unique; by its very definition, this also means that none of us are special and unique. What does that mean if every person playing on a sports team gets a participation ribbon? How many children do you know that go around showing a participation ribbon? They don't, because nobody cares. You can tell them you played on a sports team, and they may say, good for you. We don't have to reward everyone for the things they do. It gives them a false sense of self and possibly entitlement. Let them earn whatever they are trying to achieve. You don't make them better by providing answers or false praise. Teach them how to earn it. Teach them the value of striving. Teach them to be the best they can be. Life is not about trophies.

V

INFLUENCED BY EXTERNAL VOICES

External factors do not bring us happiness. We bring our happiness to everything we experience. We may feel delighted when we read or meditate, but it's not the activity itself that brings us peace of mind and joy; rather, we choose to be peaceful and joyful when we engage in these activities. Many people fail to grasp the fact that we can carry joy and happiness with us in everything we do. They don't understand why we would choose to sit still in one place for half an hour instead of doing something mindless like watching TV. The mind may not comprehend it. Instead, they turn to external distractions such as entertainment to find happiness. In reality, they are experiencing a moment of being present. When we are truly present, we experience joy because it is part of our essence, along with love.

We need to be independent of other people's thoughts. For example, if we want to buy a car, we may visit several dealers to find the best car at the best price. We feel elated with our purchase, but then our parents or close friends criticize our decision, saying we overpaid or that they don't like the make or model. Gradually, we begin to feel disappointed about our purchase. However, we were happy when we made the purchase. We can't let external influences affect our thinking. We tend to give too many unverified opinions, and they may sound authentic, but it's essential to conduct our own research and be cautious.

This is why we should bring joy and happiness to all we do. That way, others will not be able to influence us. But, of course, if everyone is happy with your purchase and you are starting to have doubts, question why you are doubtful or have become insecure about your decisions. As someone I greatly admire once said,

"Banish the doubt."

VI
UNCERTAINTY

How long can we put up with the unknown? We are anxious only because we do not know ourselves completely. Realistically, we need not endure uncertainty. Uncertainty is with us most of the time. We should embrace the unknown, similar to Christmas being around the corner, with the same anticipation of what we will find under the tree and excitement. There is uncertainty when we embark on a journey to a country we have never been to. Take those anxious feelings you have and turn them into excitement. After all, those internal feelings of foreboding are similar to excitement. Why not choose to feel excitement instead of apprehension?

Uncertainty also occurs when focusing on an event that has yet to happen. Let's face it: we have anxiety because we don't know how things may turn out. That is why it is essential to stay in the moment. Worrying about a future event (a fantasy of the mind) is unreal; focus on what is in front of you.

You are either washing dishes or putting a corporate plan together to save the company millions of dollars. Stay focused on what is presently being done. If it's reading a book, focus on the book. If you are doing something mindless such as watching television, stay with that. Everything is fine, and all else is an illusion.

12

ABOUT TRUTH

Even if you are a minority of one, the truth is the truth.

Mahatma Gandhi

I

BELIEFS

People are lazy. They don't conduct research for themselves. There was a President in the U.S. who played loose with the facts. He took what was on social media and regurgitated it as facts, even though he had numerous experts on hand to provide accurate facts. Sometimes, these so-called facts serve a purpose.

When my children were growing up, they used to ask me to give them answers to complex word problems. I could have easily given them the answers, but by doing so, they wouldn't have learned how to conduct research, understand what the problem is asking, question assumptions, and evaluate logical reasoning.

Another reason is that they may have misguided confidence in their sources. Just because a friend told them a story doesn't make it true. Many people mistake opinions for facts and express their views as if they were objective truths.

Finally, there is a danger when we don't know the entire picture. Say you have a coffee mug with different images on each side. The person across from you says, "I really like the dog on your mug." You look at your side and say, "No dog; it's a cat." Then you think, "What a dummy." They can't tell the difference between a cat and a dog." The truth is, neither has the complete picture. Both then tell the world that the other person doesn't know the difference between dogs and cats. They provide examples. I was sitting there looking at the cat (or dog), so I knew they couldn't tell the difference. Of course, the conclusion drawn is based on a partial view and is entirely wrong. Now, all those who had been apprised that this person can't tell the difference will tell their friends, "This guy is an idiot; he can't tell the difference between a dog and a cat." And they will quote their friend as proof.

II
TRUTH

Beliefs are based on other people's stories or experiences. We do not possess others' experiences because we were not brought up the same way. Even children living in the same household were brought up differently. Watch how we are programmed. I have been involved in many forms of communication. One illustrates how people perceive information, and I am sure the readers are probably aware of this exercise; twenty people are in line. The facilitator whispers something into the first person's ear and tells them to pass it on to the next person by whispering into their ear. When it gets to the last person, the message is so distorted that it doesn't resemble anything like the first person heard.

The first book of the New Testament was Mark, which was written 40 years after the death of Christ. Now I have friends, and my relationship is entirely different from other friends with the same person. We see things differently, and we interpret things differently. We accept information without verifying any of it, other than a friend of a friend saw such and such. Vanilla only tastes like vanilla because we have labelled it as such. Even if we saw some things that happened, our version may differ in why or how the other person (Christ) did what they did. Through their filters, the apostles then decide how and why Christ did those things. Christ may have stopped to alleviate someone's pain because He felt sorry for them. We simply don't know. Besides, two siblings experiencing the same situation come up with two different stories. It happens.

A former prime minister of Canada, Jean Chretien, once stated, "A proof is a proof... and when you have a good proof, it is proven." It is not in conflict with what Mahatma Gandhi said about truth. The truth is that which is correct 100% of the time. The sky is blue because it is blue. That is the truth of the matter. Physics describes it differently, with light refracting through the atmosphere, causing it to be blue based on the qualities of the specific wavelengths. If you are not a scientist, don't make out to be one. Leave the descriptions to them. We cannot claim its truth if we have not personally studied such matters.

A tree that falls in the woods when no one is listening makes the sound of a tree falling in the forest when no one is listening. That's the truth of the matter. We try to explain it logically. Because a tree makes noise when it falls, the logic of the question is, of course, it makes a sound. However, we can only verify it because of our own ears. If you leave a tape recorder or a motion-detecting video, you still hear the sound with your ears. If you have never seen a tree fall in a forest, how can you possibly know what that sound is like? Because you believe it based on the sounds you have heard from someone or somewhere. This is the sound of a tree falling. You may have seen the tree falling on television, so you equate that sound with a tree falling.

Finally, close your eyes and really believe there is a cobra in front of you. With all your tools available, just imagine it there. Hear the sound; imagine it coiled in front of you. Believe it is really there. Open your eyes; was it really there? No! But you believed it was.

There is only one truth. The rest is made up. We think telling someone they are ugly or good-looking is the truth. The reality is neither; both are opinions. There is no such thing as "my truth." There is only "my opinion" or "my perception." When we add adjectives or adverbs, they no longer resemble the truth. For instance, I don't like meat because animals are cruelly treated. No, I don't like meat because I don't like meat. We cannot possibly know all farmers or how their animals are treated. Criminals are evil people. That is not a truth; that is a judgment. Criminals are criminals; by definition, we have given the word "criminal." meaning. We provided that label to a specific group of people that do not follow our laws. Again, it is a label. The crimes they commit may be considered heinous, but in fact, they are crimes that we have determined to be crimes. They have nothing to do with the truth. The truth is, they committed an act, robbed a bank, killed someone, etcetera.

Agreeing on something is not always possible. So we look for solutions that someone can work with or support. That requires suspending our belief system long enough to hear the other side without judgment fully. That takes practice because, for so many years, we have done the opposite. We wait for someone to finish talking to give them our point of view or belief; we don't really hear the other person. Then, the person may get frustrated because we are not hearing them. Just think how much listening is going on when we listen to people trying to talk over each other. That becomes the real issue.

Listen to a morning talk show where there are a couple of radio hosts. They talk over each other. They also do this with the people they are interviewing. They don't really listen; they hope you are.

13

RELATIONSHIPS

Without respect, relationships are lost. We're all different, and if someone can't value your differences and respect your values and belief, then they don't deserve a front-row seat in your life.

Unknown

I

CONTROL

A long time ago, I was in a relationship that compounded the dynamics because we were not financially well off and needy. The problem is that a marriage or an affair cannot be entered into when each has needs that they expect the other person to provide. Regardless of the situation, a relationship should not be entered unless one is wholly complete emotionally. We cannot expect or monitor our partners to ensure they pull their weight. People are different, and they approach things differently. Imposing our standards, especially in a marriage, should be a non-starter.

What we tend to forget sometimes is that people change. We all change, and what we find critically important today is of little consequence tomorrow. I remember hearing someone complain that their wife had changed from when they first went out. I should hope so. First, as we gain more information about life, we tend to look at things differently. When children come into the equation, that changes people even more. Sometimes, people can't handle the changes that result from that. For instance, emotional upheaval ensues when one partner enters a relationship because they need to seek love from the other person, and the other partner doesn't respond. One is no longer there to feed the other person's neediness. The result is anger, frustration, a sense of loss, and betrayal. As we grow emotionally and understand who we are, we conclude that this relationship no longer supports us through our personal journey. Someone else may come into your life that supports this journey.

When we first meet our partner, or for that matter, we start an affair, things seem idyllic. That is because there is nothing to distract from one another. There are no financial issues, no children, and you only need to look after yourself. You do not sit and evaluate the person you are with. You are not looking at faults, only the attraction. When you move in together, things change. Now you are in a position where you have to share responsibilities, which you may never have done before. You may even perceive your role as a provider, thus keeping everything to yourself, including finances. You think the relationship's importance is to provide and can't understand why your partner is upset because they do not see being a provider as necessary. They are looking for the attention they received before being married.

When I first started working, one of the people in our engineering department had married a twenty-two-year-old. He was in his early fifties. I couldn't understand this. What was an "old" man doing with a person young enough to be his daughter? And so, I asked him. He said that you could teach them many things when you get them at a young age (grooming). They are like sponges. I knew enough then to think to myself, "Wait until she gets older and has a mind of her own. She will leave him." I could only guess why this woman would want to marry a much older man. Either it was the money, he provided some protection, or she thinks he is brilliant. It certainly wasn't for his looks. In short, there were things she was lacking. It could also have been love I doubt that either one really knew what that was. Just because we have these feelings and urges doesn't mean we are in love; it simply means we have feelings or attractions. We tend to equate these feelings to love. Love is actually much more profound.

As we get older and gain a broader perspective of who we are and how society and nature work, we become more comfortable with who we are.

II
BUSINESS PARTNERSHIPS

When looking at a business situation, two people decide on a new and innovative idea. They form a company because they think this idea has great potential. One person is punctilious, while the other partner, a visionary, may not have the slightest idea of turning that vision into a pragmatic reality. They have very differing views on how the business looks going forward. One of the partners will want to research the feasibility and consumer interest in implementing the product or service. They will want to know how much return on their investment is there, and how long before they break even? The designer or big-picture partner finds this tedious and wants the product on the market. They tend to be more impatient. The pragmatic one knows that it will take a couple of years to get the product or service to the marketplace.

This relationship will not work long-term if neither is willing to see the other side. For example, I was asked to assist someone in getting their product to market. The product itself was innovative and had a certain flair to it. I took a marketing colleague along, and we agreed that this product had great potential. He told me that a known manufacturer was willing to pay $2 million for the rights to the product. We both suggested he take the offer. With that kind of money, he could spend money and research into bringing other products to market. He saw himself as an inventor. We rolled our eyes at some of his creations; others had potential but needed refinement. The differing point of view can be the strength or the very thing that kills a business. Brainstorming can lead to immaculate ideas. One point of view can lift the other if both partners understand and are not arrogant.

The person who hired us was very good at selling but very poor in business fundamentals. He loved being the centre of attention. He went to all the fashion shows and got caught up in hobnobbing with the fashion elite and Hollywood designers. He completely lost focus on the business aspect and would make excuses as to why none of these people were committed to buying the product. Eventually, we left because being in the "in-crowd." was not a business model. Besides, once we figured out that the product, at best, might sell $100,000 worth of merchandise, we figured he had to be misleading us on the $2 million offer. Initially, partnerships seem feasible. Enthusiasm and excitement can quickly turn to disappointment and even acrimony. It is important to understand who you are going into partnership with and to understand what they will bring to the company.

III
NEEDY RELATIONSHIPS

Some of us enter relationships to dominate or validate their need to be correct. These type of people usually find others who consent, so the ties "seem" to work. Then, the person's role starts to mature and understand that they have their own voice. They need to move in a different direction. People who lack self-esteem tend to look for it in others; the other person thinks they are helping the needy one through a difficult time. Now the relationship appears to be in perfect balance. Those looking to authenticate themselves will always find someone to endorse their needs. However, when the validator realizes the other person has no interest in moving forward and only looks for their energy, the "validator" may move on.

Relationships are built for many reasons; most purport to be for love. Sometimes, a person believes they are in love, yet they still search for the solid thing. Have you noticed that when someone says I love you, they wait for the echo to return, "I love you too?" If we need to hear those words echoing back, what is really going on is not "I love you" but "I need you!"

Saying, "I need you to respect me," or, "They disrespected me," should tell the other person that they lack self-respect and are looking to validate the respect through you. However, this is only in certain cases and does not apply when it comes to any sort of abuse. In such cases, it is essential to voice our feelings and be heard.

Whatever the issue, we must all decide whether we want to enable that person or not. The mistake we tend to make is thinking we can change them. Change always comes from within and never through someone else's attempts to change them. We are never the same. I have heard people complain that their partners have changed, but they don't see themselves as having changed either. In some relationships, sparks fly when two people are at a crossroads and they believe they are passionately in love. However, it was only a crossroads. Both parties were going in different directions. Where they met was a juncture, not necessarily on the same path, although it may have felt like it at the time. If the crossing on the road is wide, say five or ten years wide, the relationship looks fine until you get closer and closer to your destination.

Not all relationships are destined to be forever. Some religions and other institutions sell the notion that marriage is forever; it is not realistic. If that is the ideal, then the ideal would be that people do not marry until they are complete within themselves. That is, they will not need anything from the other person. Of course, by then, it may be too late to have children. So there is a bit of a trade-off.

I have been married for 39 years, and while we have different aspirations, neither of us felt we needed to change each other. We are happy within ourselves and bring that happiness to the relationship. Out of all the things, happiness is the strongest thing that is evidently inward. It comes with content. Those who search for happiness from external sources, be it constant validation from their partner, would have a tough time being happy. Many years ago, I stopped working on the relationship and looked at all that was wrong. We nearly broke up, but we were willing to renew the relationship and start looking at it as when we first met. Now, we bring that into daily practice. Each day is like the first day. We "date" each evening. We are "empty-nesters." While the children were home, we never lost sight of our relationship. We included our children in everything. But our children were not our sole focus. We like each other and enjoy our company, including the children's. Relationships sometimes tend to focus solely on the children. However, children grow up and move on. What's left? The love for each other needs to stay constant. But more importantly, respect. These two factors should be endorsed to live peacefully with each other.

IV
AFFAIRS

Affairs are illusions that eventually wear off. Two things usually happen when you have an affair. First, you will notice that you become far more critical of your partner. You may think they do not know you are having an affair, but because you are connected beyond the physical, deep within themselves, they know something is amiss. You may notice that by watching your partner's attitude towards you. You think it is them; therefore, you add additional judgment upon them when it is you.

Since you are cheating, you search for the same mindset in them, despite it not being there. However, you look hard enough and contemplate evidence that is entirely made up. Your assessment is critical to having an affair, and it is the justification you need to step beyond your existing relationship.

Then there is that whole issue of keeping your word. It is the only thing that everyone has to offer equally, regardless of status. You have to decide whether the vows were a lie or if you meant them. When you were dating your partner, you obviously had feelings for them. Probably the same ones you are now infatuated with, the other, your classmate, co-worker, friends, or friends of your spouse. Maybe they are prettier or younger, but that all fades away, so what will you do, change partners in perpetuity?

Part of the reason I also say that affairs are an illusion is that they are rooted in fantasy. For instance, when you "date," there are only the two of you with no cares in the world. You have no financial responsibility towards each other, and you don't have to worry about support, raising children, and the myriad of responsibilities that come with marriage. The cliché is apropos in that the grass always seems greener on the other side. There are various sides to everyone, and one unlocks one after the other. Some of these aspects are not necessarily pleasant. However, it is up to us on how we cater to these un-pleasantries of the other.

If I may make a suggestion, look at your spouse as if for the first time. Remember what that was like? Take ownership if the marriage is failing. See what you can do. Marriage is a life-long project, and you need to work at it. Marriage is not a 50–50 proposition; it is 100% on you because that is your commitment to the relationship.

Look, nothing says you have to have the same goals. You can be a liberal or conservative, Republican or Democrat, living in the same household. It has been done before. Support each other and make it your mission to make the other person feel better. We made a pact not to go to bed angry with each other. It doesn't always work, but we are one hundred percent committed to resolving issues and not letting them fester. That is when the relationship starts taking hits.

V
DIFFERENCES

Relationships, by their nature, are different, and the people in them are diverse, coming from different upbringings and experiences. You must respect them all. So when reading this, it is not about the other person but you, the reader.

An emotional upheaval ensues when one partner enters a relationship because they need validation from the other. When one of them is no longer there to feed the other person's neediness, the result is anger, frustration, and a sense of loss. Their sense of security is lost. As we grow emotionally and understand who we are, we conclude that this relationship no longer supports us through our personal journey. Someone else may come into your life that supports it.

I have heard people complaining that their partner nags them all the time. What are they nagging about? It is usually something that has not been taken care of. Dishes in the sink, toilet seat left up, frivolous spending, a light fixture that needs repair, or a ceiling that needs fixing. The reasons for "nagging" are endless. You need to look at yourself in the mirror and address your partner's complaints. They are advocating their voice, and you need to be the one who is supposed to listen. Your commitment to them owes it.

If your partner is harping on how you handle (or don't) your finances, perhaps you need to look at that. If there is an issue with how your children are raised, maybe we need to look inward and ask, "What is best for the child?" Mostly, I have seen parents get angry at children because the child is whiney or angry or doesn't want to eat what is being served.

Parents are frustrated because they are looking for their children to obey. They fail to realize that the child may have a different view. Their individuality validates them to say no and nag, then it becomes a power struggle. Parents mostly, but not always, have the best information. How often have we heard the phrase, "I sound just like my mother/father?" There is a reason for that. Have you programmed yourself based on your parent's upbringing of you? After all, what kind of role model did you have for parenting?

VI
PERCEPTION OF MARRIAGE

There are so many ideas and notions about marriage. We have cartoons, films, religious institutions, and parents to help us form our perceptions. Marriage changed my perception of marriage. I knew that it was a partnership, but only to an extent. Each of us still needs to accept 100% responsibility for the relationship. I used to think marriage was a 50–50 responsibility; you always look to the other to pull their weight. I lived on my own for many years before my marriage. I learned to look after myself, cook, clean, etc. I was a complete person within.

I was not searching for any validation from my partner, so when I entered marriage, I could be 100% responsible for the relationship. I didn't need anything else; I was not needy and didn't need to be loved. I already loved myself, so I could give my love freely and not listen to the echo when saying I love you (I love you too). I didn't need my wife to respond in kind, although she does.

I had outstanding teachers in my parents; I had never seen them separating household duties. My father made soup because he was good at it, and my mother would cook other things. They came from different cultures and barely spoke each other's languages, but they made it work. My father would clean the house when my mother was at work, and my mother would tackle one room at a time once a month and thoroughly clean it, including drapes, moving furniture, and washing walls and ceilings.

The essential thing in a relationship is that we don't always need to be correct. In marriage and by watching others, we discover that we all have different perceptions of experiencing the same event. Our minds are unique, and the perspective formed over one event is based on the unique aspect of every individual. Therefore, there should be no right or wrong. If your partner squeezes the toothpaste in a way you disapprove of, buy your own. Stop complaining. If your partner wants the toilet seat down, then do so; it is not worth arguing about. Re-evaluating one's annoyances can do wonders. We must remember that we are always the common denominator when angry or annoyed.

Therefore, it is us that must change. Stop having to be right! If a man points a gun at you and says you need to give him your coat, you can argue that the coat is yours. You may be correct, but you also may be dead. Would you rather be right or dead? Take that philosophy into your relationship. Would you rather be right or alone?

VII
SEX

A few years ago in Ontario, the schools changed their curriculum regarding sex education. (A new government rescinded many of those initiatives.) While many in the province supported sex education, several religious groups were opposed.

Their position was that it was up to the parents to teach their children. All well and good, and had they done so, it may never have found its way into the school system.

Some feel uncomfortable talking about sex to their children. Those with prejudices and shame instilled teaching that caused separation from those who do not share their philosophy.

It creates tension because not everyone shares the same knowledge or has access to the right information. Thus, homophobia is allowed to flourish. While sexual feelings are vital at a certain age, they are misconstrued as love instead of an expression of love.

Sometimes, sex is not about an expression of love either. It could be about power, control, or addiction. I am not a psychologist, so I can't begin to theorize about those aspects, as I have only read about them. As mentioned earlier, these opinions are solely mine, based on my own experience and without much research. Long before becoming a parent, sexuality played a big part in my life. The difficulty then became how to translate that into guidance for my children. Worse still was the fact that I had all girls. So, would I teach them to avoid boys; they can't be trusted? Why not? First of all, I didn't know "all" boys. Their intentions may be noble, but they still wished to have sex.

Some children have been brought to believe sex is evil and they should not under any circumstances engage in intercourse unless it is to procreate. On the other hand, some fathers who were very strict with their daughters were very promiscuous. I'm not sure how they square that, but I think it may have something to do with relating to other women as objects and lesser beings. How else do you force your children to be celibate while simultaneously pleasuring yourself with women nearly your children's age in some cases?

I never learned about sex at home, nor, as I recall, did many of my schoolmates. We seemed to pick up from older kids a year or two ahead. Of course, they were much more knowledgeable about these things than our parents.

I have no idea how old I was when someone told me about masturbation. I tried it once, based on the description of a friend of mine. It didn't work, so I returned to him and said it didn't work. He said you need to keep doing it; eventually, it will come (pun sort of intended). So, back to the bathroom I went, determined to find out what masturbation was all about. The second time it worked. The feelings and sensations that came overwhelmed me. I had never experienced anything like it before, so not only did I discover the best toy ever, but the pleasure I derived could easily have become an addiction. Fortunately, there were sports, books, and television to keep me from being consumed by those unique feelings.

I realize that sex and religion seem to be intertwined. From the religious aspect, it was a sin to waste sperm without the intent of having children. Seriously? I can't recall who first said that masturbation causes blindness. The joke was that we would stop once we needed glasses. I guess that explains wearing glasses. Oh well, an enjoyable experience. I maintain that if God didn't want us to enjoy sex, he would have put that "tool" out of reach. Even monkeys enjoy masturbating, I'm told.

So, back to what to tell our kids, not much, unless they ask. Because they were girls, they discussed these issues with their mother, who was also not a prude when discussing sex. Sadly, many still learn about it in the schoolyards or in the back alleys, in worst-case scenarios, movies or porn. This warped sense of sex had me applauding with approval when I became aware of our government's change to sex education, much to the resistance of churches and other religious groups.

Even right-wing politicians got into the act, saying that teaching sex is the parent's responsibility. Isn't that how sex got to be so dysfunctional in the first place? Sadly, when they changed the government, they changed teachings much more to the liking of the religious right. Children deserve proper teaching of this natural act in a sound, scientific light. The more taboo this topic is made out to be, the worse things will get.

VIII
PARENTING

How often have you heard the saying, "They didn't give you a manual for parenting?" There is a reason why people say that. You cannot expect every human being to react to the same stimulus. I chuckle when people claim how a child must be raised. Really!? We must engage with our children.

We have to know and understand them. That is the exciting part about being a parent. Expose them to as many things as you can possibly afford. Introduce them to new cultures, religions, people, and anything you can think of to expand their minds. Let them discover who they are. They could only do this if they could access sources to aid them. I believe parents must teach by example, not only by word.

Don't be surprised if children pick up some habits from their parents. Don't worry about not getting it right. In my experience, it matters not if you get some things wrong, so long as it comes from a place of love and compassion. Allow yourself the pleasure of having your children teach you a thing or two. Personally, I became a good leader because of my children. They taught me how to lead. I took this with me when I started supervising. My children taught me non-judgement, love and compassion.

I don't advocate homeschooling, but I understand where some parents come from. Those that want to teach for their own prejudicial reasons should be stopped. Yet, where do you draw the line? Are we not all pre-judging what is right or wrong to impart to our children? I mainly question homeschooling because it takes away social interaction with others. By the time a child reaches high school, they already doubt themselves, from looks to social behaviour to acceptance. That is difficult to teach at home if there is no context to hold the information.

Certain aspects of social interaction are necessary for personal growth. Sometimes it means being bullied or getting insecure. It teaches one a lot about personal growth and patience. These cannot be taught or experienced being homeschooled.

One thing that schools and parents don't teach is how to have children control their emotions. Schools can't do it. By telling children to calm down, they think that this somehow teaches them to quieten their feelings – not so. Parents can't even control their emotions, much less teach their children to do so.

Thus, we get angry and selfish children who become angry and selfish parents, and the beat goes on. We propagate these notions through the way we communicate. "You make me angry,"; "You make me feel happy,"; "You make me feel sad,"; "You make me feel…" (feel free to fill in the blank).

Yet when we analyze our own feelings, what is the common denominator? It is never the other person but us. Ultimately, we decide how we feel and who to blame for our feelings. We learn from childhood, from our parents usually and reinforced by our relatives and friends. This allows us not to take responsibility for our own feelings.

Why not look at why we feel a certain way? When someone says something that "makes" you angry, what is the trigger within us that causes us to feel that way? Why can two people hear the same message, yet one gets angry, and the other takes the statement at face value with no emotions attached to the statement's reception?

Similarly, have we looked at our partner's "shortcomings" to reflect on our triggers? If your partner does not see their shortcomings, perhaps your perceptions should be reviewed. That is not to say that partners do not have weaknesses, especially if they are abusive or constantly see the negative side of life. Then it becomes their issue. If that is you, then you are still the one with issues.

I noticed that we want to keep children in a sort of bubble. Oh yes, we want them to experience everything we did growing up, only to do it in a controlled environment. We do it in order to protect them, but in reality, we are stealing away the very experiences we want them to have.

Take sports, for instance; when I was growing up, there were very few organizations where kids could play baseball or football. We used to find a free diamond and play pick-up baseball in the spring through the fall and then switch to football in some parks. Some switched to hockey during winter because a benevolent father would make an ice rink in their backyard. In one case, the father of a boy that no one seemed to like for some reason used to go to the park and create a sizeable hockey rink.

This was done with a lot of care and pride. Many used the rink but with very little appreciation for the effort that went into it and maintaining it. Personally, I never cottoned up to the game. It was just too cold outdoors. (Now we have indoor arenas). By the time I laced up my skates, my toes were frozen, and it just didn't seem like a lot of fun. Besides, I could barely stand up on those two blades. Who invented such a silly game anyway? Oh dear, so un-Canadian. I preferred baseball and football. There was a lot less running around in either sport. This was mighty convenient, yet still fun. It was why I didn't play much basketball either. When playing football, and if you were lucky to be around a high school with a regular football field, sneaking onto the field made us feel like professionals.

The changes between the sixties and now seem to have shifted towards organized sports. It appears that some parents believe that their children will become professional athletes through participation in these organizations, while others think that it is a safer option.

Nowadays, I observe many kids playing organized soccer, and the days of sandlot baseball seem to be a thing of the past. Parents are partially responsible for this trend as they sometimes shout at the referee or coach, putting their children in an embarrassing position when a decision goes against them.

Personally, I preferred the informal games because there was no pressure to perform. We played simply for the fun of it. We would go to the park, and anyone with a bat and ball would join in. We were too poor to have our own equipment, so we relied on whoever had it. Since parents did not attend these pick-up games, there was no pressure to play in a specific way. We had a good time and developed our own skills without any interference from a coach or parent.

As we grew older, some of us progressed to organized sports. I recall a team I used to watch, which had two excellent players. One of them was a catcher who was drafted by the St. Louis Cardinals, and the other was a first baseman who went on to have a Hall of Fame career with the Montreal Alouettes. Children my age had the space to learn and grow at their own pace. They did not have their parents dictating their every move to lead what they perceived to be a fulfilled life.

I have several nephews; some played organized hockey from a very early age. What surprised me was the venom these parents showed towards the coach, the referees and even their children when a poor decision was made, a blown call or a child simply not where he was supposed to be. I wonder whether some parents think that their sons are meal tickets to professional sports. Why else would you turn a fun game into such severe reactions?

On another level, I shouldn't be surprised. I started off coaching in a children's baseball league. The emphasis was for all children to participate, regardless of how good they were. I had children tell me what position they wished to play, and some parents insisted that their children play certain positions. I had one sad sack individual who clearly had never played baseball before. I guess his parents wanted to involve him in sports. There was pressure on me to win from the parents as some of their children had from the organizing committee to ensure everyone played at least three innings.

When you have fifteen people on the roster, something must give. The poor chap that played right field saw many balls sail over his head before reacting. Of course, this caused more groans than the pitcher that gave up the run. That poor boy did not have a great experience in playing ball. The kids ostracized him because he had never played before, and I suspect his experience was not there. I gave him credit for persistence; by year's end, he could make some catches in the field. I congratulated him on each good play or hit. Encouraged him to keep himself constant. I did not do it; fortunately, neither did the league give them a trophy or participation medal. That, to me, was the worst thing we could do to children. Reward them for something they did not achieve (win) and have them avoid disappointment.

Whoever said being disappointed was a bad thing. It motivates to do better. I realize that not everyone can win. In the end, there is only one winner. That does not mean the rest are losers in the negative sense, but it is a means of assessing oneself and the team to see that everything possible was done. Beyond that, hold your head high, knowing you have done your best. The rest is really not in your control. The only thing you can control is if you have fun.

My other experience was when I was coaching in an industrial league. I soon discovered that even adults could be like kids. Initially, they would tell me what position they preferred to play before evaluations. Later, they would approach me and ask for playing time or for an at-bat. I even had an opposition catcher tell me that I was giving a signal to steal a base at different accepted counts. This person had all the skills and talent to be an excellent catcher, but their mind got in the way, and I understood why they were playing in an industrial league. The reality is, if you can exploit a catcher's weakness to steal a base, you take it, regardless of the count, unless opening first base compromises your best hitter's chance of hitting. Partway through the season, a father approached me and said he wanted his son to pitch for us. He thought it would be a good experience, and he was too young to get into an older league. I had him try out and demonstrate what he could do. He impressed me enough that I took him on. Besides, we could use another pitcher at the time. He was not pitching effectively in one game, so I replaced him with our other starter. Unfortunately, the following pitcher got shelled. Had I done the logical thing of putting the young pitcher at first base, I could have left him in the game and perhaps brought him back when my other pitcher was faltering.

On the other hand, you don't need a sixteen-year-old to blow his arm out. While the team forgave my boneheaded move, the kid's father never did. He screamed at me and did everything but hit me, and I am sure that the thought had crossed his mind. I got it. It was a season-ending mistake that caused us to miss a run at the championship. The following year, his son played for another team on another field. His father made a point of travelling across the entire park to let me know in no uncertain terms that I screwed up, and that he had taken his son to a better team, somewhere he was appreciated. This carried on for the whole new season, usually with his son in tow. I thought to myself, I'm glad he is not my father. If he could carry such hatred for a man he didn't know over a mistake, I would hate seeing how he reacted to his wife and children.

This happens when a fun game turns into a grim, humourless event. Teaching children to be good human beings should trump any necessity for winning. The inability to let go of events is a serious flaw within us humans. Our institutions may house people who cannot let events or experiences go.

In a series of books called "Conversations with God" by Neale Donald Walsch, Neale stated that grandparents should raise children. Even though I am a father and raised my children with my wife, I know the value of raising them with grandparents. They have a better perspective on life. They are more experienced, making them wiser. Some things can only be taught by our wise old birds. I also chuckled when I read that, as I thought there was no way I would want to raise my grandchildren. As much as I adore them, I prefer this time to be about my wife and me instead of worrying about raising our grandchildren.

The idea, though, is relatively sane. For instance, grandparents are not in the habit of proving that they make good parents and that to do so looks like being strict and having them behave in a certain way. They are not embarrassed by the child's behaviour, so they would not be inclined to do anything to keep the child from having a tantrum in the supermarket.

I took my cue from my mother, a nonjudgmental woman who embodied motherhood. There were times when she would tell you in no uncertain terms that our behaviour was unacceptable, but mostly a particular look was all it took. I was a product of the fifties and sixties, so t-shirts and jeans were the fashion of the day, Haute Couture, if you will. Anyway, coming home for Christmas one week and sitting down for a meal before dressing for Christmas Eve, we sat around the dinner table, and my mother casually leaned over to me and stated, "I thought we raised you better than that." That's basically all it took. It woke me up to who I was and the statement I made with my clothes, which was inconsistent with the person I aspired to be.

I ran a coffee house in the mid-seventies for about a year. It was the type that had musicians playing on the weekends and amateur nights on Wednesday evenings. A musician whose name escaped relayed a story about living in an apartment alone. He had just taken a hit of acid a bit earlier, and the effects were starting to kick in. Just at that time, there was a knock on the door. As he opened it, there was his mother. He immediately slammed the door shut in a panic. Realizing he couldn't leave her out there, he let her in. Her reaction was to say, "Why is your face falling off?" Well, that sent him into another panic as he rushed to the washroom to check for himself. That, to me, is a remarkable parent. No lengthy lecture about the evils of drugs, just a pointed observation that made an impact. A concerned mother asking about her son in an orderly fashion.

My children have been a valuable source of pride. They are unique, yet they all exhibit love, humour, and compassion. I really misuse the word pride here because I apportion pride to something we have accomplished. At best, I may claim to be an example and provide the space to develop into beautiful human beings. The rest was up to them.

Our parents always want the best for us. They view what is best for us from their knowledge lens and perspective. Many parents without the time or privilege of education are stuck with what they know. They see sitting for an hour, seemingly doing nothing, as a waste of time. Reading, too, is viewed as spending time fantasizing. Some people think everyone should be busy all the time. I knew of a mother who didn't understand it was essential to have their children educated. All in all, everything a parent does is for the utmost betterment of their children. They all wish to see their children strive for greatness.

My father was a teacher and a military officer. He came to this country after the war, not speaking a word of English. He tried to convince my brother and me that we should be engineers or doctors because these were transferable skills used in any country. He saw this as necessary because he thought he didn't have those transferable skills. (I could have coached him on those, but the real issue was not transferable skills; it was language.) His strength was in leadership, as was practiced in the military during the forties and fifties. My brother was a rock and roll musician with a master's degree in music, subsequently earning a doctorate in education. I dabbled in Industrial Engineering for about seven years before running plants which was much more rewarding, and later doing arbitration cases.

I am sure I disappointed my parents in many ways (sometimes, parents have expectations when children are small, so it turns out to be a disappointment when they don't entirely turn out the way they expected). We argued over many things, including my grades, leaving school without completing high school, ignoring curfews, and generally being a pain in the ass.

My dad endured all this because it was done with love. His life had changed radically from being a person of privilege and then becoming a general labourer in this country. That was hard. He wanted his kids to have conveyable skills so we would never have to endure what they did. That is kind of hard for a fifteen-year-old to grasp. After all, parents don't know what we know at that age. Ultimately, we had to find our paths, regardless of how difficult and painful that may be. After an individual is unique, they have a mind of their own, which moulds the way it was intended to. Parents have a certain say in their children's development but do not have a full grasp on their minds. We all tend to have pictures of how our children will turn out. In reality, our children (including us) turn out to be precisely the way we should. Our life experiences will be different from our parents' experiences. Therefore, parents placing impositions or expectations on their children does not produce teachable moments; instead, they may cause them to deviate from their destined path.

I was fortunate to have my father live with us for ten years before his passing. We completed our relationship, and my children were also able to connect with him, making a difference in their lives.

14

LIFE

Life isn't about finding yourself; it is about creating yourself.

George Bernard Shaw

Many people have a significant impact on our lives, even if they are unaware of it. We seek out individuals who have something to offer us, but we often do not recognize the extent of their influence. One person who comes to mind is Werner Erhard, the founder of est. While he was aware that he made a substantial difference on a large scale, his impact on an individual level was perhaps less obvious.

He had a profound effect on my life by causing me to perceive things differently. Despite being criticized for running a cult by some and having zealous followers by others, his message was that we were already fine the way we were and needed only to recognize who we truly were. He suggested that our fears were primarily based on illusions and that we were not alone in our feelings.

This realization had a significant impact on me. It took time to absorb everything and realize that we were all connected. I came to understand that when we criticize someone, we are actually criticizing ourselves. This can be difficult to accept, especially when our ego is involved, as we tend to perceive the problem as external to ourselves.

I remember thinking how preposterous the suggestion was that we created the world as we know it. We are a part of it. We can't help it if someone in China wants to explode a bomb in North America. That can't come from us.

The first thing I thought about was what happens when we die. Well, the world as we know it will cease to exist. Others will argue that it doesn't; after all, we have witnessed many people dying, and the world as we know it is still here. Of course, it is because we are still here.

So, it stands to reason that our world has not ended. I wonder how much worlds are connected, but at the same time, not at all. When a person dies, his world has ended, yet it still goes on for others (in most cases).

What drives our world is our insecurities, pettiness, righteous positions (our need to constantly be right), our view of right and wrong, good and evil, etc. While I am aware of all these diverse issues globally, they are not part of my world. In other words, I have not fallen victim to them. The moment your thoughts change, so will things around you.

Religion teaches us not to judge others, yet at the same time, it can pass judgment through its dogmatic positions. We cannot compare people to religious teachings and judge them accordingly since no one is perfect.

People have justifications for their actions, and as judges, we do not know what those justifications are, making it impossible to make accurate assessments. Only after understanding the motivations behind someone's decisions can we suggest alternatives. In the past, I, too, made the mistake of labelling people as right or wrong.

However, after focusing on what drives and motivates people, I became more compassionate. Even in movies, when the villain's origin story is explained, their actions tend to make sense, though they are undoubtedly wrong. The point is that everyone has a reason for what they do, and those who don't are labelled as psychopaths.

Only a small percentage of us want to find out why we are on the planet, our contribution to being here, and how we fit into the rest of society. It is important for one to know themselves and then know their purpose on this planet. When we are guests in someone's house, we do not defecate in their living space nor leave the place in a mess of our own doing when we go. This is simple etiquette.

Why do we not do the same with our planet? After all, we are like guests; we stay for a relatively short time. Instead of spewing pollutants into the air, we should try to remember to clean up after ourselves as a guest. We should appreciate and follow the indigenous community regarding the environment.

They know how to take care of it. Instead, we dismiss them as savages and essentially rape the earth of its resources and pollute the environment. Even when it is pointed out that we are creating an unsustainable planet, we continue using jobs and the economy as an excuse to continue adversely impacting our environment.

I

PREJUDICE

Where does the act of pre-judging people we don't know come from? How do we direct so much hate toward them, sometimes even to the extent of wanting to harass them and offend them with physical violence? We tend to want to marginalize others so as not to see our shortcomings. Perhaps someone has told you that someone you have known has made a remarkable achievement.

We may then agree with that person and have a "yeah, but" behind that. "That individual has done an outstanding job. She has produced more than any other employee." Response: "Yeah, but she is always late." Note that one has nothing to do with the other, but for some reason, people are compelled to add something that diminishes the person's achievement. It all comes down to competing, even when it is unnecessary.

I realized a long time ago that prejudice resides in all of us. The more we become aware of our biases, we can eliminate them by looking at what is right with people and situations versus what is wrong or what separates us from "them."

I used to think that the British were arrogant. Where did that perception come from? Listening to my parents and deriving my opinions from newspaper articles about what politicians were saying. I also had a low view of Indigenous people.

This came from friends who had an encounter with one or two; thus, my opinion formulated that they were all drunks. In addition, the newspapers had written articles on individual Indigenous people being arrested for drunk and disorderly conduct. When a grade twelve English teacher asked me where I got the information from, I simply said, "Well, it is all around you. Just look at the newspapers." Of course, as I started to think about this, I began to realize that all the Indigenous people I knew were of high quality. Yes, I ran into some on the streets of Saskatoon and Regina who were quite drunk. If I was looking for confirmation of my earlier views, then for sure, I would have more proof. I made it my business to find out more about our first inhabitants. I soon discovered that many were in pain because of residential schools. In addition, our government did not honour many of the treaties. We threw some money at them, hoping that the issues would disappear.

Yet, in 2023, we still have not addressed many land issues. Some still cannot get clean drinking water. And only now are we starting to make restitution regarding the infamous residential schools. Judging or labelling a person or even sects of people under one pretense is easy. However, only a fair individual would search for the underlying root of the immoralities.

I have many friends who arrived from Great Britain after the war, and none of them reflected the attitudes of their government. I realized that we could not pre-judge people just because of what we were raised to believe, and our parent's premises were wrong in some cases. Or perhaps the times and people were much troubled at their time.

Today, we are more familiar with various people, some even countries apart. We are learning to respect the differences and cultures of each other, mostly thanks to the internet and social media. Regardless of our thoughts, whether with people of a different colour, those from other countries, or other geographic locations, we simply don't know them all. Therefore, how can we possibly judge people? No, we can only assess those we come in personal contact with. We must put our thoughts aside and simply listen, regardless of whether someone is angry or uses language to which we object. Not everyone is educated the same as us, nor do they have the same life experiences.

When I travelled through India, I came across desperately impoverished people. These were the poorest of the poor. Generally, in society, they are dismissed. We look at them from our point of view. That is, we have been privileged enough to grow up in a community with a stable household, an education, and three meals a day, then we wonder what is wrong with them. We look on our own streets and try not to look at the beggars on the corner.

Why? Are we too embarrassed to engage them in conversation? Then we say, get a job, or "I don't give them money because they are simply going to buy liquor." We have no idea how they get there. We assume things in the majority of people. Judging an entire group of people because a couple were degenerates. One person I met was a high-powered executive in a tower in the financial district. Something happened, and from one day to the next, he was sitting begging on the streets. He abandoned his house. His family offered him to stay at their house, but that wasn't the issue. For whatever reason, he would not be confined in a place. If it had not been for social workers taking an interest and getting him the help he needed, he might still be on the streets.

It's easy to make assumptions about someone based on their appearance or behaviour, but we don't know their full story. We know that those different from us or act differently are all human beings, and we do not know or understand what pain or suffering they have been exposed to. We don't know what they've been through, what challenges they've faced, or what trauma they've experienced. It's not our place to judge them without having walked in their shoes.

It's also important to recognize that mental illness and addiction are not choices. They are illnesses that require treatment and support. Calling someone lazy or an alcoholic only reinforces harmful stereotypes and ignores the root causes of their struggles.

Instead, we should approach everyone with empathy and compassion. We should seek to understand their experiences and offer support where we can. By doing so, we can help diminish our own prejudices and create a more inclusive and understanding society. It's up to each of us to do our part in treating others with kindness and respect, regardless of our differences. As humans, many carry burdens. Treating them with compassion instead of contempt will also diminish our prejudices.

15

POLITICS

Too bad that all the people who know how to run the country are *busy driving taxicabs and cutting hair.*"

George Burns

I

POLITICIANS

"If a political party does not have its foundation in the determination to advance a cause that is right and moral, then it is not a political party; it is a conspiracy to seize *power."*

Dwight D. Eisenhower

Everyone seems to have an opinion on how to run a country. Those with incredible egos may be driven to run for politics. Oh yes, some start out with the purest of intentions, but do they really think they have all the answers? Unfortunately, the country cannot run by itself, so we need someone to represent us.

Ironically, those who aspire to represent us often have a hidden agenda of seeking power and control. Their focus on representing us takes a backseat. Their primary argument is that without being in power, implementing changes is impossible. This becomes their driving force for seeking power. Their strategy is to prioritize winning the next election rather than serving the people they represent. It seems that their tactic is to tackle all the unpleasant tasks in the first two years of their term, followed by spending the next two years winning back the public's support. Ultimately, the entire game plan is centred on devising strategies to retain power for as long as possible. What's wrong with saying, "Here is our platform, and this is what we think is best for the country; if you agree, vote for us; if you don't, don't vote for us?" Politicians should look at what is best for the country and its people, not necessarily what people want.

It is impossible to run for political office without being criticized; they are savaged for whatever they do or fail to do. Look at what we do with our politicians and world leaders. Every opportunity we get, we try to bring them down. We look at what they have not done versus what they have accomplished. There seems to be a "yeah, but" attached to whatever little praise we offer. Mostly, there is no praise. The mindset mainly comes due to unhealthy competition between the rival parties. They instill negative thoughts in the minds of the civil people in order to portray the evil incentives of their opponent parties.

I listened to a discussion on allocating money for bicycle lanes. Right away, the ones with the cars were lamenting how we spend money on bicycle routes instead of road widening. Others complained that they should have done it sooner. A small faction also claimed it was too little too late. Those are the ones that really have nothing to add to a conversation. Why do we do that? It is never too late! We must start somewhere.
To say we should have done that ten years ago is a fool's game. We could not have done it ten years ago because the circumstances were different. Everything happens at its own pace. If politicians are not convinced that the population is

ready, it won't happen, regardless of whether it is correct. There are protest groups on both sides of the spectrum that rail against people and politicians who think they can resolve any issue. Unfortunately, name-calling and swearing at decision-makers usually have the opposite effect that protestors demonstrate. You cannot teach or convince people with anger. Those who demonstrate should know that anger doesn't work. People tend to tune out when yelled at, or worse, they absorb their anger, resulting in scaling up the rhetoric or turning to violence. Think back to how you felt when you were yelled at, be it by the teacher, parents, or friends. My advice to protesters is to run for office. If you are not elected, move on; people disagree with your point of view.

II
TAXES

Politicians often seek to cut taxes as a popular policy among voters, but it's crucial to understand that taxes fund essential services. If we were to eliminate taxes, we would have to eliminate many necessary services that people depend on. Let's eliminate an army that only exists because of obligations to our allies, the United Nations and NATO.

Who is going to invade Canada, and for what? The most likely country would be the United States, as they start to run out of water and other natural resources. Next, let's get rid of all the social programs. Who needs them? The rich can look after themselves, the middle class can get them from the employer, and the poor are always forgotten.

We can give them some spare change at the corner they work. After all, even in Mathew 26:11, Jesus is attributed to saying, "The poor you will always have with you...." Some religious communities use this quote to justify enormous wealth rather than sharing it to feed and educate the least in our society

Advocating for reducing taxes is generally from the conservative viewpoint. When I look at politicians elected to minimize taxes, the first thing they do when elected is reduce taxes, which results in deficits. Then they turn their attention to cutting services that affect the least of our society. Those living on the margins never benefit from tax reductions. This is done to win the immediate vote of the people. Most are tone-deaf to the services the taxes provide. They fail to understand how a country mainly runs on these taxes. The politicians, on the other hand, despite knowing the detrimental effects cutting taxes will have on the country's economy, do it anyway. Why? To stay in power, of course.

The conservative-minded cut taxes and increase military spending. They never explain how they plan to reduce the budget while increasing military spending. This little caveat about lowering taxes seems enough to get them elected. Of course, they can claim that they were elected on that platform. If there are inefficiencies, politicians are the least likely to find them.

Leave that to the people that run the departments and hold them accountable. We should do what is best for the country. The conservatives always claim that they are fiscally responsible and that those liberals created wasteful spending and deficits. Yet when the other party gets in and cuts taxes, they do so when the country is already in a spending deficit. Why do that? Wouldn't it be more logical to reduce spending and then cut taxes?

For instance, if you found $1 billion in savings, then perhaps cut taxes or, better still, pay off the debt by an equal portion. Just because it may take three years out of the four-year mandate to get that reduction, should be no reason to cut taxes before creating those savings.

We can argue that cutting taxes stimulates the economy (a favourite argument of the right). Increase spending to kick-start the economy (the darling of the left). When we look at the results, the evidence seems to point at the economy picking up or declining despite who is in office; it seems to have more to do with timing than economic philosophy. Both sides take the credit and shift the blame to the other party.

Let's cut taxes on the middle class and increase them on the wealthy. That is always popular, as the majority think they are in the middle class and the rich have lots of money. True to a degree, but realistically, how many wealthy people are there? Unless you tax them somewhere between seventy-five percent and ninety percent, it almost isn't worth it. Unfortunately, we are stuck with the middle class. There are more of them, and we don't have to tax them as heavily as the other class. Who likes paying taxes? It is necessary. If we don't look after our poor, who will? The easy answer to the poor is that old refrain, "Get a job," or you should have gone to school. Then there is the belief that if we throw enough money at a problem, it will go away. We fail to reason how a country works, more importantly, how the economy works. Cutting taxes without direction could lead to long-term problems for short-term gain.

III
WASTED RESOURCES

The next politician I hear talking about how they will eliminate waste has really lost my vote. They are not telling the truth. Those in power have had a chance to reduce government waste since at least the late nineteen fifties. Opposition parties are not changing the world. They want to get elected to positions of influence, and then they'll try to figure out how to do everything they promised. Knowing climate change is the people's biggest concern, and they use it to gain their votes. They are fully aware that their promises concerning climate change control are incomprehensible. The reality is there is waste everywhere. Resources are wasted; there is a lack of accountability in spending; we build something to have a shelf-life so the economy can survive. The government plays a part in keeping the economy going. Businesses waste, too, despite waste reduction policies. An area of tremendous waste is our natural resources. Canada and many African and South American nations have almost limitless resources. Yet, instead of manufacturing them into a saleable commodity at home, they ship them out for other countries to benefit. Depletion happened at a much faster rate than if the sourcing countries had developed their own raw materials. This was the short-sightedness and wasted opportunities of both government and industry.

IV
TRANSPARENCY

We tend to focus on the effects rather than the root causes of issues, which is something wise politicians understand; how else to constantly point out the symptoms and then offer the cure pill? They often highlight the symptoms and offer solutions, as getting to the root cause of problems can be tedious and not newsworthy.

It requires a lot of effort and may not produce visible results for many years. Elected officials should be transparent about the time it will take to address issues and provide a roadmap for the population at large. While there may not be total agreement or consensus, at some point, a decision must be made, and an explanation should be provided. Politicians have a limited time frame to work with, and people are often impatient.

Regardless of how long they have been in power, governments that serve for too long are subject to change. The opposition tends to focus on the negative aspects of a government's actions rather than acknowledging the significant positive impact they have had on people's lives. In the United States, a president can only serve a maximum of eight years.

A CEO once told me that failure is not the be-all-to-end-all; what's important is the batting average. If a government is batting .700, that would be acceptable in most areas (of course, not all, a surgeon with that kind of success rate or an airline pilot with a similar score would be disastrous). What do we demand from our politicians that we don't require of our work habits? Imagine making a mistake, and suddenly you have your entire office around your desk yelling at you for being such an idiot. See if you become stressed. We all know that we do not always think straight under pressure.

We wonder why they are not transparent. A child will hold the truth from their parents because of perceived consequences. An adult or politician is not much different. (We learn what works from early childhood and continue to use it until it no longer works.) The consequences are that they may lose their jobs over some mistake. I remember working in a toxic environment where no one wanted to tell the truth. The CEO of a large national company was involved in the minutest detail of a worker's miscue on a line. That CEO wanted to fire a twenty-five-year employee with an unblemished record because he dared to commit an error.

As a result, most senior management, recognizing the consequences of telling the truth, preferred not to speak and devised imaginative excuses for why things were not how they were supposed to be. It became obfuscation at a level also seen in politics.

We are humans and prone to lapses in judgment; we make mistakes. Someone once said, show me a person that doesn't make mistakes, and I'll show you someone who does nothing. Mistakes are what make us human. Setbacks and mistakes help us to grow in a way nothing can.

I marvel at the reasons politicians get into serving their country when they take such abuse once elected. It is not just that they are criticized (and sometimes with good reason) but done with such venom and hate. How were people raised to harbour such hatred? Those same people unleash that venom when something doesn't fit with their view of the world. My philosophy tends towards thinking that people who criticize others are deflecting from being scrutinized for their failures in life. They are able to unleash their frustrations on the politicians because all their mistakes are out in the open; also because it is easy to criticize someone anonymously.

V

POLITICAL CORRECTNESS

A relatively new phrase that has come about over the past few decades is "political correctness." You can still hear people bemoan politicians, pushing "political correctness." I have a completely different take on this. I prefer simply "correctness." We have seen the phrase P.C. as a thing to be shunned. What is wrong with being polite? First, only the completely ignorant do not know that the naming of "Indians" mainly came from our founders, who thought they had landed in India and have since called the Indigenous that. So, we shouldn't refer to First Nations as "Indians." Of course, it also transformed into an expression of a lack of respect. I am saddened by people that cannot respect the sensitivity of others. The reason I do is that they have no self-respect.

After all, you cannot give what you don't have. When you think about someone claiming to be disrespected, they are generally disrespecting others. It is also an indicator that they have no respect for themselves. You can only give what you have. If you have no respect for yourself, then how can you give anything but disrespect to others? People see in others what they harbour within themselves. Famous is the quote, *'Beauty lies in the eyes of the beholder,'* meaning that if someone sees something beautiful in others, it is because something beautiful resides in them.

We like to blame people that are different for all our own shortcomings. To suggest we have turned the corner on prejudice is a fallacy concocted by some politicians. When the left was in power, it was unacceptable to voice anything discriminatory. So, the racists learned to keep a low profile and invented a more socially acceptable communication method. Once we elect far right-wing politicians, they will become emboldened in their lack of tolerance for anything different. Some politicians are astute enough to recognize that most of the population does not tolerate this behaviour, so they distance themselves somewhat, telling their followers to tone down the rhetoric; otherwise, they may not get re-elected.

We have failed to adequately educate people about the differences that exist in our society. Throughout history, different ethnic or religious groups have been targeted, including Indigenous peoples, people of colour, Polish, Irish, Germans, Catholics, Jews, and currently, Muslims.

This prejudice is not unique to one country or religion, and the minority group is often subjected to bullying and violence. By attacking those who are different from us, we are essentially admitting that we cannot accept those differences. Even within our own countries, there are regional disparities. We may point to others as being worse, but eventually, we will become the target ourselves, and there will be no one else to blame.

Anger abounds on both sides. Those that hold prejudices are angry toward politicians and left-leaning socialists for taking up for minorities. The left-leaning socialists are mad at those that are prejudiced, yet the biases are the same; the difference is only the target. Why don't we transmute all that anger into something useful, such as building affordable homes for the homeless, providing shelter or schooling people on how to sustain themselves in this society? Instead of spending money on bombs and guns, why not spend that money on medicine, schools, reforestation and so on?

Anger has not resolved much from my short stay on the planet and what historical books have outlined. It has led to violence and death and caused many families anguish. People fail to control or counteract their anger, especially in a beneficial way. That is the root of all evils and of the strongest.

The word "Amigo" in Spanish is a male friend. The Mexicans have come to dislike this term when used by Americans or non-Spanish-speaking people. It has become a bit of a derogatory term because their neighbours to the north used it condescendingly at times. So, when one person used the word Amigo and found the recipient to lecture him on the use, the other person was offended. "Why can't I use this word? It is a legitimate use to identify someone as a friend. If they are offended, that is on them and not on me." Why would you want to offend that person if they are friends, especially since they told you it is offensive to them? We can rail against "political correctness" or fix it and respect other people's wishes.

VI
POLITICAL PARTIES

Wouldn't it be far better to eliminate different political parties? People would only get to select the best people that are running in each riding. In Canada, we have an "opposition" party. The official opposition party is the party that came in second during the election. Well, guess what they do? Their name implies it – oppose. People must adhere to the party line on many issues instead of voting for what is best.

In the United States, I have watched Republicans oppose most things a democratic President has put forward, sometimes for no reason other than being a Democrat initiative. Likewise, when Trump was elected, the Democrats opposed virtually every piece of legislation he tried to pass. Both parties are guilty of supporting dumb initiatives just because their party initiated them. These parties work by bringing the other one down in the eyes of the people. They will not give each other constructive criticism but instead, bash without logical reasoning. Such acts only spew hatred between the parties and their supporters.

In many Canadian cities, there are no party lines. While philosophies may swing from left to right or anywhere between, the point is they must work together to get things done.

Humanity has not progressed to the point of passing legislation by consensus, and that is a shame. There are people that, for whatever reason, are on their own agenda. I worked for a director who did things by consensus. We didn't always agree with the solutions but agreed that they could be supported. Sometimes the answers may not be the best, but let's go with that if they move things forward. Brainstorming ideas and ideologies could lead to better results.

The country's leader should be picked after the elections by those elected. The results may be startling. Unlike in the U.S., the speaker in Canada is selected through a vote by all parties, not by the party in power.

On a completely different note, politicians tend to check with companies about legislation that may affect them. Rarely do politicians ask the consumers or the electorate what their thoughts are. And even if they do, it is usually to tick off the box that says we consulted with them.

A business will almost always be on the side of profit, and that's what they are supposed to do. They have to stay in the game and be better than their competitors to maintain a profit. Can you imagine a large corporation saying it will reduce its earnings to become more affordable to consumers? Shareholders would never stand for such a decision. The Board of Directors would quickly remove those audacious enough to voice that kind of opinion, never mind trying to implement such an initiative.

Businesses operated for years on the premise that the greater the demand, the more they can increase prices. That boils down to greed. Of course, the shareholders are pleased. In my late teens, the post office lowered their stamps to 2 cents at Christmas, the busiest and most demanding time. If they followed the logic of big business, they might have raised it to 15 cents. At 2 cents, many that would ordinarily not be able to send cards now can send four or five for the same price as one. Is that the reason the Post Office lost money? The Post Office lost money and business because they were inefficient, had poor management and provided poor service. That is how the courier business was born.

VII
SOCIALISM VS. FREEDOM

I watched with great interest the debate Americans have regarding "social" health care. Heaven forbid that someone gets medical care if they cannot afford it. Is this not an entitlement? When did we decide that people who, through no fault of their own, cannot get first-class medical treatment to the same degree as someone with the financial wherewithal to do so? The sad part is that many of the same people who have nothing are the most vociferous in making sure governments do not meddle with these socialist notions of providing health care to those that need it and not only to those that can afford it. Another vocal group seems to be the religious right. What religion teaches you to kick those who are least fortunate? No, capitalism does not need to change; it needs to return to its roots. It needs to recognize that we are all on this planet together.

Protectionism is not the way to go, nor is greed. Let's ensure that countries such as India and Somalia have an equal chance at selling their goods along with numerous poorer nations. They, too, occupy this planet. We must learn to live in harmony with equality, or the world will succumb to wars and destruction.

Capitalism, Individualism, and Consumerism are all romantic notions of true freedom that do not exist. The other "isms" (Socialism, Communism, Humanism, Liberalism, and Nationalism) seem far scarier because they point to a loss of freedom. To protect each other, we need to curtail freedom so that people can't do as they please. Society put laws in place from the era of the Wild West; we moved to protect those that couldn't defend themselves. That may be a loss of freedom at some level. Freedom is in people's minds, and they determine what freedom is for them. If they can no longer live the way they did in the mid-eighteenth century, they may need to move elsewhere or accept the consequences of not keeping up with societal changes. It is not only people that change but so does society. That's because people make up a society.

We bring fear into politics using an "us against them" mentality. Muslims are terrorists, Blacks are violent, South Asians smell funny, and they can't be trusted. Gun laws haven't changed. Handguns have one purpose, and that is to kill. They were designed for easy access in the early 1800s and are now designed to be concealed. People will argue that handguns are for the protection of the individual. If no one made handguns and banned them worldwide, there would never be a need to carry or own one of your own. In Canada, and I suspect in some other countries, weapons must be locked in a safe cabinet. So, it would be useless if you were being burglarized and your gun was locked up in a basement locker. Even with a permit to carry a weapon, you wouldn't have a chance when a gun is pointed at you. The firearm can lead to a false sense of security. The amount of permits you need in order to keep it makes it fairly useless to have it around. Don't worry; governments monitor every financial transaction in the name of safety, phone companies monitor your whereabouts by telephone, drones can follow you home, and "security" cameras practically in and on every building will keep you safe. You also lost a considerable amount of freedom.

The press is a source of information, reporting on government and the world. There is little media freedom in China, North Korea, Eritrea, Saudi Arabia, Ethiopia, Azerbaijan, Vietnam, Iran, Myanmar and Cuba, the top ten countries lacking press freedom (source: Committee to Protect Journalism). Then there are countries not in the top ten but also limiting press freedom, such as Mexico, Venezuela, Honduras, the Americas, most of the African Nations, The Eastern European block and almost all of Asia. Some are not as bad as those mentioned, but they also have press restrictions, only to a lesser degree.

The press has been much maligned in the United States, that bastion of democracy and free speech. It now ranks 23rd among the free press, and Canada, which is not much better, is ranked 18th. Political leaders tend to blame the media for bad publicity. In recent years, the press has been undermined by "Fake news." They are accused of falsifying the news in order to gain more audience and, therefore, more reach of their channel. The competition among these channels is so drastic that they end up moulding the news to make it spicy. Much of it is floating around the internet. We tend to think that is real news, while newspapers that are far more credible than some things seen on the internet are the ones that people in authority undermine.

Ranked number one, Norway, followed by Sweden.[1] These countries are much closer to democracy and freedom than the United States, yet we look to the United States for press freedom and democracy. Without freedom of the press, there is no true democracy. Russia, Iran and Zimbabwe hold elections but are not considered democracies. The United States positions itself as the world leader in democracy. They do so because of their myopic view of the world and their spin positioning themselves as such.

Let's face it, free speech is never free, and consequences are associated with that freedom. If not directly or indirectly, a lot gets at stake when the freedom of

---

[1] Freedom of the Press 2017 and World Press Freedom 2018

speech is fully exercised. Try using unfounded, derogatory or inflammatory language against someone. You may soon find yourself in court and most likely quite a bit of money out of pocket.

We tend to see politicians talk more and more about homeland security, and I am not necessarily talking about U.S Homeland Security but security to whichever homeland is yours. Politicians claim they can keep you safe, which is nonsense; most of us know this. They play a role in keeping the audience engaged with themselves in order to win their votes. But those who fear their shadows are willing to sacrifice freedom for security. At what point do we say liberty is more important than security? At what point do we start drilling down to the root cause of the stealing, looting, violence towards women and our war-like mentality to address some of those issues instead of worrying more about locking people up and more surveillance?

On a similar note, I wonder if privacy is overrated. I say this only because I wonder how people's behaviour would change if everyone knew what everyone else was doing. Would a person watch pornography, for instance, if everyone knew they did? Would politicians make deals with land developers if everyone knew the developer's or politicians' true intentions? We are all grateful that no one knows our business at times. After all, if everyone at the office thinks you are a great guy, and then you go home and abuse your wife, I'm sure that your colleagues would have a different opinion of you. Without privacy, perhaps everyone's behaviour may change. Having others think of themselves as good and noble is more important. The question is, will not having privacy make things better or worse for people in general?

When people say, "This is my country," they have a false sense of what ownership is. We have the same regard for furniture in an office. "That's my desk;" "You're sitting on my chair;" "That's my pen." None of these things are yours, except perhaps your pen, unless it was a company issue. The owner is the company you work for.

Similarly, the country is really owned by the residents of the planet, and it should be shared equally with all citizens of the world. Everyone should have the privilege of travelling wherever they choose. In the end, the populations would most likely be the same, except diversity would be far different. Imagine the possibilities of learning new cultures, religions, food and dress. The learning opportunities would be endless.

Politicians are responsible for erecting barriers between countries. They have promoted nationalism for a long time, which creates a sense of superiority and competition. This is mainly about power. We have identified people as different and inferior and, therefore must keep them away. Politicians have also generated fear of the unknown, and we have bought into this. We all want to belong to a group that is admired and emulated. Nationalism encourages us to compare ourselves with others. Fear can make us behave irrationally, leading to harm to others. It is easy to show compassion to those we love, but we need to extend that love to all the inhabitants of the planet. Then we can demonstrate kindness to everyone.

Other than the small factories and shops, there is no free enterprise, and even they are affected by the larger ones. Americans are so worried about socialism that they fail to see they have created a socialist system for Corporations, coined "Corporate Welfare Bums" by Ed Broadbent, formerly leader of the New Democratic Party in Canada. Look at the tax breaks they get over private citizens. Then there is government help to pay for new buildings. How many big businesses coerce the government into pitching money for new sports stadiums or arenas? Look at the bailouts of the automakers, all because they mismanaged their companies while the CEOs never missed a bonus payment. These are the same people that oppose giving individuals a break. Why can't the wealthiest pay benefits to the poorest individuals who work for places that don't provide health benefits? And why can't everyone have the same "Cadillac" benefits that all executives get? Is one life more valuable than another? Why not offer those who fail to get an education because they don't have the money or the mental capacity to learn beyond a particular point accommodation? Many corporations have their hand out for protectionism, if not financially. The concept of rich would not remain for these folks if the poor did not exist.

Are Enron executives or Anderson (who audited the books) nobler than politicians? When we give corporate executives additional incentives to perform what they were hired to do, how much extra value do they add to a company? To acknowledge a problem would mean a lesser bonus or perhaps none. How else can one explain the near collapse of the American banking system? Are we suggesting that the automotive executives who came (cap-in-hand) to Washington in a private jet are an expression of what American capitalism is about? If that is the case, it's not saying much for the system. The free enterprise belongs to those who are not on Wall Street's radar.

Indeed, a nation is judged by how it treats its least fortunate. Many religious institutions in the U.S. run hospitals (As of 2016, there were 700 faith-based hospitals (Georgia Health News)). The problem is that there are not enough of them to cover everyone. Some riders in some insurance plans are not pretty. My brother was a high school principal in the U.S. He had what many consider a very generous healthcare plan. When his wife needed surgery, she was forced to attend a hospital of the insurance company's liking. The U.S. might have the best healthcare facilities in the world, so much so that even the elite all around the world prefer visiting them. However, that is the thing; only the elite can afford their healthcare plans and facilities while the unfortunate (lower and middle) succumb to the lack of viable options. Canada may be viewed as a socialist country, but at least its citizens can attend any hospital anywhere in the country. Oddly, socialism seems to be the scourge of American thinking. Yet, many socialist European countries (Germany, France, The Netherlands, etc.) and even Canada are better financially than the Americans. I wonder why that is? The conservatives who value less government always seem to set the country back. Ronald Regan cut taxes and increased the deficit. George W reduced taxes while increasing spending; how does that work? Even our government brought the country into massive debt. The Liberal government had us in a surplus situation for years, and we happily paid down our debt. They even managed to create an emergency fund when needed. In 4 short years of Conservative government rule, they reduced taxes and increased spending, creating a 56 billion dollar deficit. There was no benefit to the poor. For tax relief to benefit people, they have to be well off enough to pay taxes in the first place. Creating deficits by cutting taxes is irresponsible. If we did that as individuals, we would be bankrupt in no time.

Before doing anything else, one should ask what they expect from their government. Less government is not necessarily realistic. Let's ask how effective our government is. Are they doing what they were elected to do? Is what they propose in the people's best interest in the long run? Reducing taxes or government without a purpose is unproductive. Why should any country ever reduce taxes before having paid off its deficit? Does that make sense? Social debates should never be based on money but on whether it is being used accurately. There will always be disagreements as to how the government spends money. Governments and private institutions are run by people. Some are good, and some are not so good. Either way, there always needs to be a goal with a plan that can be measured with people held accountable. When that happens, I'm sure we won't need to discuss capitalism versus socialism.

VIII
GOVERNING

Governments are there to look after those with the least means and opportunities. Unfortunately, there is an element that seeks power for its own sake. Having three levels of government can gridlock the system. The initial intent was good. Our forefathers never envisioned the infighting and intransigence this would cause. In fact, up to about thirty years ago, neither did anyone else imagine this.

When campaigning, politicians or political candidates promise people all sorts of things, but once in power, not so much. It becomes about party discipline and what is best for the party, not the people. In politics, I often hear, "We need to do this to be re-elected so we can do the things people elected us for." Instead of doing what they are supposed to do, they continue to do things people will re-elect them for instead of what they are supposed to do. Politics has become a mere game of power. As stated, whatever these politicians promise to do or act on is only a façade to get re-elected in stay in the privileged lane as long as possible.

What's wrong with saying, "Here is our platform, and this is what we think is best for the country; here are the ways we will prioritize these initiatives; if you agree, vote for us; if you don't, don't vote for us." Politicians should look at what is best for the country and its people, not necessarily what the people want or, for that matter, the politicians want.

It is impossible to run for political office without being criticized; no, savaged for whatever they fail to do or do. Look at what we do with our politicians and world leaders. We try to bring them down at every opportunity and look at what they have not done versus what they have accomplished. There seems to be a "yeah, but" attached to whatever praise we offer in everything we say.

Not all initiatives are popular, and not everything will be aligned with their base. But if they do what is best for people instead of themselves, in the long run, it will work out. I tend to look at a politician's batting average, which never speaks to me entirely when I look at the party's platform. I must accept some things I disagree with for the overall platform which may resonate with me.

I get tired of all the people who find something to complain about regardless of the party in power. And those that do complain are mostly complaining about their interests. If they are so outraged with the government, then run for office and make changes.

Americans have a history of violence against governments, starting as far back as Abraham Lincoln. Therefore, it should be no surprise that January 6th continued that violence. At least, if they run and don't get elected, they can understand that the majority do not go along with their ideas. One can never take from people what they don't want to give up by force; that's called stealing.

So many of us complain about the taxes we pay. Why is the government constantly increasing taxes? Some politicians feed off this and pledge to reduce taxes. All is well and good, but they never see where they can come up with savings. Let's face it; we would be in a pickle without taxes. Who would pay for the military? In our country, we have health care paid for. No one has to worry about selling their home to save their life. Where would you be without roads, bridges, or public transit? These are things that take taxes. Have you ever noticed when politicians pledge to reduce taxes by streamlining existing programs, not once do they offer to reduce their salaries by the same percentage? Hmmm, why is that?

IX
CAPITALISM

Our perception of capitalism can be distorted at times. We may still cling to the romanticized notion of Henry Ford and other entrepreneurs who wanted to create quality products at a fair price while providing their workers with enough money to afford to buy the products they produced. However, some large corporations operate less as capitalists and more as socialists who despise socialism. Governments from all nations were quick to intervene in the rescue of banks and the automotive industry. If capitalism was truly thriving, wouldn't we allow these companies and institutions to fail naturally? After all, they nearly went bankrupt due to greed and mismanagement. We rescue them because it is what society expects of the government. We love capitalism, except when it affects us personally, in which case socialism becomes preferable. And how about the subsidies that governments provide corporations so that their industry moves to their jurisdiction. Where does free enterprise fit into that scenario?

We are so hung up on our own "isms," and everything else is wrong.

Shouldn't the government's role be to protect the least in our society? The idea is not to throw money at those who are not working or less fortunate than us but to put them on an even footing to have equal opportunities as the rest of us. Some intelligent kids will never see the inside of a college because they cannot afford it. Some do not have what it takes to go to college but may have other skills that should be pursued. We leave them to fend for themselves. What is wrong with ensuring they get a fair chance at life too? It is not their fault that they were born into low-income families or lacked the skills to attend university.

I watched with great interest the Americans' debate on "social" health care. Heaven forbid that someone gets medical care if they cannot afford it. Is this not a right? When did we decide that people who, through no fault of their own, cannot get medical treatment to the same degree as someone with the financial wherewithal to do so are somehow less important? The sad part is that many of the same people who have nothing are the most vociferous in making sure governments do not meddle with these socialist notions of providing health care to those that need it and not only to those that can afford it. Another vocal group seems to be the religious right. What religion teaches you to kick those who are least fortunate? No, capitalism does not need to change; it needs to return to its roots. It needs to recognize that we are all on this planet together. Protectionism is not the way to go. Let's also ensure that countries such as India and Somalia, amongst other poorer nations, get an equal chance to sell their goods. They, too, occupy this planet. To bring this discussion home, capitalism should not be about the ability of people to pay. It should be about setting a fair price. If you can increase production and lower costs, pass the savings on to your employees and shareholders. If all you are focused on is profits, then you just become greedy. I have read that some CEOs had fudged their profit margins to claim their bonuses. That is a total regard for the employees that worked for the company. One CEO told me that her biggest concern is the employees that work for her because they depend on their paycheques.

Capitalism, Individualism, and Consumerism are all romantic notion of true freedom that does not exist. The other "isms" (Socialism, Communism, Humanism, Liberalism, Nationalism) seem far scarier because they indicate a loss of freedom. The news flash is that freedom was lost a long time ago, and George Bush, and later,

Donald Trump, in the name of freedom, reduced the freedoms of America even further.

We bring fear into politics, using an "us against them" mentality. Muslims are terrorists, Blacks are violent, South Asians smell funny, and they can't be trusted. We have white people with guns viewed as one-offs; how else to explain that gun laws haven't changed? Handguns have one purpose, and that is to kill. They were designed for easy access in the early 1800s and are now designed to be concealed. People will argue that handguns are for the protection of the individual. If no one made handguns, and they were banned worldwide, there would never be a need to carry or own one. In Canada and, I suspect, other countries, weapons must be locked in a cabinet. If you were being burglarized and your gun was locked up in the basement, it would be of no use to you anyway. Even if you have a permit to carry a weapon, you probably won't have a chance to get it out if someone already has a gun pointed at you. The weapon can lead to a false sense of security. In the name of safety, governments monitor every financial transaction. Phone companies can monitor your whereabouts by telephone; drones can follow you to your home; we have "security" cameras practically in every building and street. You may feel safer, but you have also lost considerable freedom.

The press is a source of information on what is going on in government and the world. It has been much maligned and persecuted lately. There is little freedom of the press in Russia and China, and everyone acknowledges that. Turkey has joined the Arab States in controlling the free reign of the media to the point they no longer provide free-flowing information.

In the United States of America, the press has been much maligned, that bastion of democracy and free speech. Presidents tend to blame the media for the bad publicity they get. In recent years, the press has been undermined by "fake news." There is much of it floating around the internet. We tend to think that it is real news, while newspapers are far more credible than some things seen on the internet, are undermined by people of influence and sway.

.

X

FREEDOM

In a song written by Kris Kristofferson and Fred Foster (Me and Bobby McGee), one of the lines was, "Freedom is just another word for nothin' left to lose." In some ways, this may be true. Who are the primary people complaining about freedom? Are they not the ones that are afraid that the little they have to lose may be their freedom?

For safety, we want to ensure that our property and person are safe. To do that, we have to give up some freedoms. Otherwise, we don't have autonomy; we have anarchy. There seem to be some that would prefer that; it thins the herd, so to speak.

What is freedom really? Where does it exist? It must be in our minds because we all seem to have different concepts of what that means. Perhaps a faulty program is at its source.

Are there degrees of freedom? What is right next to the limit of your prerogative to say what you wish to express? For instance, at the forefront of free speech is that you should be able to say whatever you feel without repercussions. Well, does that include lying? Does that involve playing loose with the facts? Many politicians seem to play loose with facts, and that seems acceptable. That is, of course, unless you are outright lying. In that case, you may be subject to a defamatory act. Some of the craziest arguments for free speech come from racist organizations. Some jurisdictions now have limited some dialogue by differentiating "Hate Speech." The point of all this is that there is no such thing as "free speech." I remember an older gentleman telling me that there is no such thing as "free." As a youngster, I didn't know exactly what he meant. He explained that the item purchased came with a free cup of coffee. In reality, the item's price covered the cost of the coffee. So it really wasn't free. Fast forward a few years, and I realized that freedom is also related to life. For instance, there are consequences for every word or action we take; some you may agree with while others may not be to your liking; very little is free; one way or another, we pay; payment could be direct or indirect.

The problem is that there is an element in society that thinks there should be no consequences for your actions; that would be true freedom. Unless, of course, it happens to them. Recently, Canada had a demonstration against COVID restrictions and inoculations against the disease. They demonstrated in residential neighbourhoods, blaring horns and creating noise from 2:00 to 3:00 am. This was done in the name of freedom. So, if I parked a tractor-trailer in front of their house and started blaring my horn, I would imagine they would not be pleased, even if I told them it was my right to protest their protest.

We look at dictatorships and say their people lack freedom. There are many people in the land that do not care. So long as they can earn a living and generally be hassle-free, it is all they need or want. Revolutions come and go with little change other than you cannot decide on your fate when promises are not kept.

We say that governments are far too intrusive in our lives. Yet we complain when things are not run efficiently. So, the complaint is whether your government is judiciously spending your tax dollars. That is a different argument from an intrusive government. We don't want immigrants, yet the economy is not sustainable without them. The smaller the population, the greater the tax burden on individuals. Instead of complaining, we should be grateful for coming here and contributing to society.

How much freedom do our indigenous communities really have? We have taken their prime real estate, herded them into unsustainable land and then complained about them. We should thank them for using the grounds we live on, allowing them to continue as stewards of the land. They can be trusted far more than the people now in charge. In Canada, pockets of indigenous occupied lands require boiled or bottled water in 2022.

We have put rules in place and restrictions upon people for safety reasons. Most citizens know that they have given up a measure of "freedom" to be safe, and safety is a priority for most people. Some people prefer not to be vaccinated against transmissible diseases; vaccination is essential for the vulnerable among us; thus, we require citizens to be vaccinated. Schools in two provinces in Canada require students to be immunized against certain diseases. We have eradicated polio and tuberculosis through immunization. Slowly, cases are creeping up again, all because an element in society refuses to be vaccinated.

16

LEADERSHIP

"If you want to make everyone happy, don't be a leader; sell ice cream."

Steve Jobs

I

LEADING

I chose the quote from Steve Jobs because not everyone will agree with your approach or personality. While leaders must be compassionate and understand employees, that doesn't necessarily mean they will be liked. Leaders must express a vision of what needs to be done, then step out of the way to let the employees do the work.

I started my leadership role at the tender age of twenty-one. Before I took over the department, the previous supervisor had been there for over forty years. It was intimidating, to be sure. Everyone in the department had at least twenty years on me except three, who were my age. They were material handlers and ensured the machine operators had enough material to do their jobs. My previous job was in quality control, so I didn't know much about the department besides the end product. Each morning, I would receive the schedule of what was needed for the next three days.

How do I ensure that the employees would get it done or that the material handlers would get them the needed material? My focus was first on the back end to see if we were getting our product out on time. If not, I would work my way back to the machine operators, only to find out they didn't get their materials on time. Back to the material handlers, they seemed to be engaged, but not entirely. When Raw material arrived, it was just dumped into the aisles or on racks. There was no rhyme or reason for how they were organized; thus, the material handlers took a lot of time to find the necessary materials. We worked together to create a semblance of order so they would know precisely where materials for a given order were stored.

I discovered that people knew what their job was, but when dealing with employees with no formal training and left to their own devices, they would figure things out according to their knowledge. To be efficient, you must be organized and define what is required and why. In other words, you need to develop a process that can easily be followed.

. We all have the capacity to lead, but our willingness to take responsibility for others often obstructs our ability to do so. I recall coaching both an industrial baseball team and a youth baseball team, although I never saw myself as much of a leader at the time. I used to play baseball and was decent for a while, but since it was just sandlot, teaching others could have been daunting. Instead of dwelling on all the reasons why I shouldn't coach, I saw the need for someone to step up and volunteered. We played well enough, and although I made some errors, a classmate helped me teach younger players the fundamentals of stealing bases. Softball necessitated a distinct approach.

I had one of the adults steal a base on an odd count. The opposition had a catcher that fancied himself as a know-it-all, and he knew on what count to steal a base. Looking at him, you wonder why he wasn't playing professional ball. I started to understand why he didn't. He was a bit of a hothead, and I soon learned that the way to upset him was to steal basis on any count; he was easily raddled. I took advantage of that. In all matters of life, we need to be flexible. People will use it to their advantage if you are dogmatic.

Several years ago, I led a group of professionals in transition (jobless) in writing resumes and mock job interviews. A writer and motivational speaker named Robin Sharma wrote a book called 'The Leader Who Had No Title.' I purchased several of these books and handed them out. We are leaders not because someone gives us a title but because we do our absolute best in whatever we do.

This is something I also sensed when I first started working. I was never much good in school, already 18 at the end of grade ten, which I also failed. My first job was as a dyer's assistant. That meant bringing the dyes to the machine operator; we had to remove them from the vats when the yarns were bleached or dyed. The largest vat required four people to empty it, and I enjoyed being the fastest to empty them. I brought dyes to the machine operators with alacrity and generally had a good time. I got noticed, and within a couple of months, I was given my own machine to run. It was the large one we bleached dye in. After a couple of weeks, they noticed that my yarns were much brighter than they had been. I had taken the initiative to slightly alter the formula. Shortly after, they gave me two machines to run, then three. The superintendent came to me and asked if I would like to work in the quality lab. I agreed, as the alternative was to go to the night shift. (The union had started questioning why I, who had the least seniority, was on the day shift). This is to say that doing your best does get noticed. You see, I never thought that to get promoted, I needed to demonstrate I could do a good job. My motivation was to be the best I could be and have fun doing so. The rest took care of itself. I also engaged some of the other helpers to have some fun too.

II
First Impressions

Make a good impression, as the first one lasts. How many times have we heard this or a variation of this? I have to admit that I do not adhere to this philosophy, nor do I require respect. First, the notion of a good impression is subjective, and your good impression may ultimately differ from the next person. Besides, isn't it really a judgment? If you can move away from judging your employees, you may actually get to hear their grievances. They will then feel as if they have been heard. There was a fellow who worked for one of my supervisors. I used to tour the plant and say good morning to the employees. Some would take longer than others, as they had something to say. I never cut them off. One individual, whom we will call John, never acknowledged me.

Some colleagues had mentioned that he was just surly and I shouldn't waste my time on him. I continued to say good morning to John for about six months. One day, he approached me and asked if he could talk to me. Surprised would be an understatement; I said sure, led him to my office, closing the door behind him. He spoke to me about an issue he had with his family, and I just gave him my full attention. I am not a psychiatrist, so I offered no words of wisdom. He thanked me for listening, and ever since he acknowledged me when I came by. I would not have had this opportunity to engage John had I entertained my colleagues' suggestions.

I recall another incident where someone constantly put management down. One day, he didn't show up for work, and someone mentioned that his father had passed; I sent flowers to his family with the company's condolences. When he returned, he thanked me and said it was the nicest thing management had ever done for him.

It is important not to judge people because we never know what drives their attitudes.

III
CONSISTENCY

Some supervisors and managers have "favourites." They tend to treat some employees differently from others. A manager had suspended an employee for the balance of the shift. The manager stood at the entrance on the following shift waiting for the employee. When he returned, the manager asked how he enjoyed his day off. The returning employee was not amused and answered with profanity. That was enough for the manager to suspend him again. What was the purpose of all this? Did he really think that the employee would work harder? Most likely, the employee would sabotage his work or book off sick. It also indicated that he might have been overstaffed if he could afford to suspend someone so cavalierly. Sometimes, leaders forget that their employees have families, which count on their wages. It is one thing to suspend someone for a serious breach, but doing it for sport was utterly wrong. Leaders have such a crucial job. It ensures the company works according to plan and includes their employees' well-being. Ensuring the employees are respected and worthy will give them the space to use their best abilities.

I made it a point to treat people equally and fairly. If I had to discipline employees, I always heard their stories before deciding on a course of discipline. We had a campaign to get employees back to work after long illnesses or absences. There was also a great deal of pressure to keep absenteeism down. There was an individual who needed time off. His supervisor had denied the request, so he came to me. I told him I would check into it. When I asked the supervisor for his reasoning, he said the employee was not very good and had attendance issues, so he denied his leave. I explained that even "bad" employees need time off, and we should not discriminate against them just because they "were poor workers." I told him to go to the employee and submit a formal request, which will be approved. He turned out to be one of the better employees. Sometimes, you just have to show employees that you care. It is also noticed by other employees.

IV
HOW WE TREAT THE LEAST OF US

Just because someone has a lower position does not mean you can mistreat them. After all, every employee is essential because their jobs are important. Let's face it; for companies to work, we need everyone doing their job; otherwise, why have them?

After returning to the working world after completing school, my first job was in the Industrial Engineering Department of an electronics firm. Following some months, I became responsible for the maintenance department. One of the crew members was the sweeper; it was his job to keep the plant clean. He did it wonderfully. I used to see him read during lunch. One day, I asked if he had aspirations beyond being a sweeper. He told me he did not. He majored in English at university and enjoyed reading. He did not want a job that would take him away from reading, so cleaning afforded him that luxury without the hassle of answering to anyone. Here is an example of a brilliant person who understands what he wants and is satisfied with earning enough to pursue his passion. I admired him for that. I never considered him anything but a fellow human being on his own journey. He did not just go through cleaning motions; he did it impeccably well. He was what Robin Sharma described as a "Leader Without Title."

V

MASTERY

It takes 10,000 hours to reach mastery or 625 days (founded on 16-hour days) or, if 8 hours/day, then 1250 days. This equates to 21 months or 42 months. Either way, it is less than five years of dedicated time, and this is nothing.

I had the privilege of running a coffee house for slightly over a year. Many musicians came to play; they were all very good but unsung. One, in particular, was awarded the "Best New Artist as a Juno recipient." I found it odd that he had been toiling for years before being "discovered." Later, as I got to know more musicians, I discovered there was no such thing as instant success. Even the Beatles toiled for years playing smaller clubs before they burst into the North American market in 1964.

One must strive to perfect their craft, regardless of what it may be. The focus should be on practice and improvement, without getting hung up on the idea of achieving perfection, which is a subjective concept. However, this doesn't mean settling for a subpar outcome. Instead, one should set their own standards for excellence and strive to meet them. Don't worry about meeting the expectations of others; focus on meeting your own. Remember that there is always room for improvement, so keep pushing yourself to be better.

Don't let fear hold you back. You can manage it by either tucking it away in your pocket, turning down its volume, or using it to your advantage.

Seek out those things that make you uncomfortable. A friend of mine told me a long time ago that if you don't like something or don't want to do something, it is probably a good idea to embrace it. It is similar to the philosophy that if you observe the majority of people going in one direction, you should probably run the other way; that is where the rewards will most likely be. Embrace change!

Most importantly, keep moving forward. Don't get stuck in the past; it serves no useful purpose. This is a short talk on mastery, and there are many good books written on it should you wish to delve deeper into what it takes.

VI
BUILDING RELATIONSHIPS

When I started working, the notion of building relationships didn't occur to me; I just did my job. Later, when people brought it up, I realized that is precisely what I was doing; I had never articulated it before. Of course, there is a connection when you engage with people and really listen to their concerns; that builds relationships. There are many types of relationships, but the most enduring ones are those you regularly keep in touch with. People may come into your life for a short period, make a difference, and then they are gone, never to be heard from again.

Then some come into your life and stay for a relatively long period, sometimes the rest of your life. The relationships may vary. For instance, we have a friend we haven't seen in over thirty years; we stay in touch, update each Christmas through cards, and always feel connected.

My absenteeism rate was always the lowest when I was running a shift. My colleague (the day-shift manager) would always say that it is because you manage the night shift. These people want to impress others to get onto the day shift eventually. The day shift had the largest absenteeism because it was an aging population. So, shortly after I took over the day shift, the absenteeism rate began to decline. Why was that? Each day, I would make it a point to talk to twenty people so that I spoke with at least one hundred by the week's end. They did not report to me directly, but that wasn't the point. I wanted to know who they were and why they enjoyed working there. It helped me form better relationships.

There was an employee who had a terrible attendance record. The collective agreement allowed him fifteen paid sick days per year, and he took that plus several more. I asked him if he was okay. Was there an underlying medical issue that kept him away? When he responded with "no," I asked him what he was passionate about. He loved being outdoors; enjoyed fishing and hunting. "Why don't you pursue a job in guiding others?" He said it didn't pay enough. (at the time, he was making $14.50 an hour, significantly higher than the average wage). I told him that he wasn't making close to the money with all the sick time he was taking. If he needs the money, he should stay and improve his attendance. If not, then he should pursue his passion.

When I left the department, many employees got together and bought me two expensive bottles of brandy. It was greatly appreciated. One employee, however, wanted me to know that he had not contributed to the gift because I was "management." I told him that was okay. I thanked him for the great job he did; because of him, the machines kept running.

These relationships are essential to ensure employees find an excuse to go to work when they feel tired rather than calling in sick. Sometimes, when we are engaged in activities, we forget our maladies.

Many years later, I decided to open my own consulting practice. Every job I got was through referrals or relationships I had built.

VII
COMPASSION

When I started working, a typical management style would be to rule by fear. People were afraid to lose their jobs. Supervisors were in charge, and they knew everything. After all, they were promoted into this situation because they were good workers. They took their cues from the previous supervisor. They did the same thing because very few saw an employee as a human being, with all the frailties that go along with being human. When someone needs a day off because there is a family issue, let them take it. It doesn't matter if they are a "good" or "bad" employee; compassion is needed. It is an essential element that has expanded over the years in leadership roles. What you do to one employee is not limited to them; the word spreads among the others. Together, they evaluate what kind of leader you are. The compassion you demonstrate is noticed by all.

I came to a new department as a supervisor. Once a week, the superintendent decided to throw someone out; he would take pleasure in doing so. Some of his other supervisors joined in. There was no regard for the employee's financial status or emotional well-being, having to go home and inform his spouse and children that he had been suspended. Worse yet, they may not believe him when he tells them there was no reason for the suspension. After all, who would think that someone could do such a thing? Of course, the suspension would be thrown out at arbitration a year or more later. The superintendent would be paid overtime to witness the arbitration while the employee would finally get justice. This created two issues. The first was that employees did not trust management, and the other was that employees had the mindset that they would get their money back whenever they got suspended.

This led to insubordination and other disciplinable offences. Some were legitimate, others not.

I have been in a position where I have had to let many people go over the years; I never took this lightly. They were not bad people; (the euphemism of the day was to call them "rascals"); they were just people in the wrong jobs. A year or so later, one came back to me and announced that being fired was the best thing that had happened to him because he got this wonderful job. That job paid less, but he was far happier.

As a leader, I was asked, what legacy did I wish to leave? I thought about this and realized that I wanted people to feel better about themselves after interacting with me, regardless of the subject we spoke about. That is still the philosophy I go by today.

VIII
VISION

If there is no vision, there cannot be leadership. How do you follow someone that has no idea where to go? Years ago, I took over the mechanized sorting machines at the Post Office. At the time, we managed 650,000 sorted pieces per night shift, using twelve sorting machines. That was considered a good night. The first thing I did when taking over the area was to take everyone into a conference room. We spoke for roughly an hour. (Based on a seven-hour workday, that would be approximately 93,000 pieces that would not be sorted). I said I would like us to move to one million pieces per night; to do that; we would need everyone to be on top of their game. I thought doing so would be a fun achievement they could be proud of. The only way to achieve that was to work together, and if someone had to go to the washroom, they needed to let me know so they could be replaced. This was the only area the union objected to. "We are not school children" and "you cannot monitor people on how long they are in the washroom." I pointed out that it was a safety concern in addition to the reason just outlined. In the event of a fire alarm, I needed to be able to account for the whereabouts of the staff. I also needed to know if I should replace the person.

We started by moving from 650,000 pieces per night to 700,000. It didn't happen nightly, but it excited the employees that it could be done. We slowly moved to 750,000, then 800,00. By this time, no one was leaving their machines, but it became increasingly difficult as we continued to run out of mail. Even though we had a lot of buzz in the plant, we hit a plateau. I knew there was mail in the building, but where was it? I tracked the mail back to the docks. It was unloaded in a timely fashion from the trucks, but the employees who separated the mail into machinable and non-machinable left for lunch for thirty minutes. That is where the bottleneck occurred. I asked their supervisor if he could leave one person behind to continue sorting. When the rest of the crew returned, he would be free to go. There was a snag. A provision in the collective agreement stated that the employees' lunch could not be changed without the employees' permission. We found a volunteer, and within another few weeks, we reached our target. Without that vision, we would not have reached the goal, as it took the employees' buy-in. Getting employees engaged cannot be achieved by simply monitoring them but by providing them with a vision and letting them see that it is achievable. The closer they got to their goal, the more engaged and motivated they became.

When taking over another facility, I wandered into a toxic work environment. I pulled the employees together and told them that making off-coloured jokes and derogatory comments about fellow employees was unacceptable. Instead, I focused them on the work they were required to do. We focused the conversation on the importance of their jobs. I explained that people depended upon the delivery of cheques, especially seniors who relied on them. Businesses, too, needed money to operate. I also talked about the competition. For instance, Loomis, Fed-Ex, DHL, and UPS did not get their start by being cheaper than the post office. They got that way because of superior service. Customer service is key to job security. Our customers are our priority; we must remember and act that way. The toxic work environment disappeared, and carriers began to focus on what was important: the customer.

IX
CONCLUSION

To continue growing as a leader, it's important to understand that learning never stops. Once we achieve a certain level of education or expertise, we should not assume that our journey of learning is over. To remain relevant in our fields, we need to make progress and continue to learn. There are various courses and resources available that can help us stay updated in our disciplines. You don't necessarily need to go back to school; reading the latest information in your field and becoming involved in organizations can also be beneficial. Presenting information is a great way to learn as well. You can join organizations such as engineering associations, human resource associations, recycling and petroleum, or even CEO organizations if you're in charge of large corporations. In addition to learning, it's crucial to stay healthy. Exercise plays a vital role in brain function by increasing oxygen flow to the brain. Therefore, staying updated and healthy are crucial to remaining relevant and successful in today's world.

The final part of the leadership triumvirate is inner growth. You must also develop as a human; after all, how can you know others without knowing yourself? How can you be compassionate with others if you are not compassionate to yourself? You cannot love your spouse if you do not love yourself. A lack of trusting people will stifle any innovation. Growth starts from within; only then can you prosper outwardly.

ACKNOWLEDGEMENT

This book is dedicated to my wife, Norma, who helped me grow as a person.

I would be remiss if I didn't mention my parents, who have left this reality for another.

I also want to acknowledge my wonderful children, who taught me far more than I could ever teach them.

Throughout the years, these people have made a difference in my life; they changed my perspective on how I view the world.

Thanks to Carl Grindstaff, Walter Grasser, Janie Randolph, Nicole Goodfellow, Chuck Reece, Trish Barbado Ali Chakaroun, David Munn and Karl, my first supervisor, who has since passed but taught me everything about leadership.

ABOUT THE AUTHOR

Arno Ilic has experienced many things in life that have brought him to certain conclusions of how life works in general. He invites you to read this book, but most importantly, he does not want you to add the information as another piece of information to be added to the computer. Rather, he would like you to evaluate what is being a writer, accept those parts that resonate with you and discard the rest. Arno is not attempting to change your mind or think of him as some kind of guru or spiritual leader. The whole idea of this book is to raise questions within yourself. They may be the uncomfortable ones.

You can visit Arno's website ilicmanagement.com and follow his Facebook page by the name of Arno Ilic Author.

www.ingramcontent.com/pod-product-compliance
Lightning Source LLC
LaVergne TN
LVHW091214080426
835509LV00009B/982